WHY SHOULD I GO TO PARIS

WHY SHOULD I GO TO

PARIS

THE CITY YOU DEFINITELY
NEED TO VISIT
BEFORE YOU TURN 30

THIS IS WHY!

Paris is a classic. The City of Lights offers the perfect mix of iconic landmarks, stunning architecture, and abundant culture. Each *arrondissement* has its own atmosphere and charm. Montmartre, at the foot of the Sacré-Cœur, feels like a bohemian village, but when you stroll along the Champs-Élysées, you get a sense of the metropolis that Paris is. Quartier Latin has an intellectual vibe, whereas Le Marais is full of *boutiques* and well-dressed locals.

Visiting this vibrant city doesn't have to break the bank. Explore the different areas, take in the scenery, and soak up the atmosphere. Walk, cycle, and use le métro, rather than taking expensive taxis. Book a nice hostel, join free walking tours, and visit the famous sights and museums. You don't have to go to the top of the Eiffel Tower to appreciate its beauty. Have a picnic along the Seine or the Canal Saint-Martin and immerse yourself in the local culture.

This is a city where culture, cuisine, and fashion converge. Visit an exhibition, indulge in freshly baked baguettes and buttery croissants, hunt for vintage treasures, and have an *apéro* to end the day. Or learn some French, purchase a new novel, and relax in one of the green chairs dotted around Jardin du Luxembourg. Paris offers a myriad of experiences for every taste and budget. One thing is certain: you will want to come back for more.

CONTENTS

Bar des Quais

DISTRICTS

Paris is divided into twenty numbered *arrondissements* (see page 43). You can tell the location of an address by the last digits of its postcode, which show the arrondissement number. We'll list the coolest Parisian areas below. Some of them cover multiple arrondissements.

Montmartre

Montmartre is a picturesque neighbourhood located on a hill topped by the Sacré-Cœur, the beautiful basilica overlooking the entire city. The area has an artsy, village-like vibe with its narrow streets, charming squares, and colourful artists. It breathes creativity and has a nostalgic charm that is very attractive to visitors. Montmartre is not only known for its artists but also for lively markets, cosy cafes, and breathtaking views.

18
17
19
8
9
10
2
3
1
4
11
20
7
6
5
12
14
13

Pigalle & Grands Boulevards

Grands Boulevards offers monumental architecture, grand shopping centres such as Galeries Lafayette, and the majestic Opéra Garnier. Pigalle is all about its nightlife and has always been known as the entertainment hub of Paris. Together, Pigalle & Grands Boulevards offer a mix of fun, culture, and stunning buildings.

Quartier Latin & Saint Germain des Prés

In Quartier Latin you'll find historic narrow streets, Sorbonne University, and a lively student population. The district also houses the Panthéon and the energetic Rue Mouffetard. Saint Germain des Prés is known for its galleries, boutiques, and the Jardin du Luxembourg. Both neighbourhoods have a charming atmosphere, with cosy cafes around the Odéon area.

Le Marais, Les Halles & the islands

The heart of Paris is formed by Le Marais, Les Halles, and the islands, Île de la Cité and Île Saint-Louis. You'll find a mix of charming boutiques, selling from the smallest labels to the biggest brands. Le Marais is known for its Jewish and LGBTQ+ communities, making its atmosphere diverse and lively. And this is also where you'll find historical landmarks such as Centre Pompidou and Notre-Dame.

Belleville & Ménilmontant

The emerging working-class neighbourhoods of Belleville and Ménilmontant are known for their neighbourhood cafes and charming shops with a focus on organic and eco products. The proximity to Père-Lachaise cemetery and the picturesque Parc des Buttes-Chaumont adds even more character to these vibrant neighbourhoods.

Bastille

The Bastille area is loved by those who enjoy a bustling nightlife. With an abundance of bars, clubs, and restaurants, the atmosphere at Bastille is always energetic. The district also is of historical significance, with Place de la Bastille as a reminder of the French Revolution.

Tour Eiffel, Champs-Elysées & Concorde

These iconic landmarks are among the most visited places in Paris. The Eiffel Tower is a world-famous symbol, while the bustling Champs-Élysées and Place de la Concorde are known for their beautiful architecture and luxury shops. These neighbourhoods offer a mix of grandeur, culture, and entertainment and are a must-see for every Paris visitor.

PRACTICAL INFO

GETTING AROUND

Paris really isn't that big, and many iconic landmarks are within walking distance of each other. But nevertheless you'll cover a lot of distance, so bring a pair of comfortable shoes. Walking will always be the best way to explore a city, but there are more ways to get around.

Navigating the city is a breeze thanks to the extensive public transport system. The metro's network is efficient and speedy, which makes it a quick way to travel around Paris and easily move between various districts, landmarks, and attractions. You never have to wait long for the next train, which makes them popular with commuters as well as tourists. Use the Bonjour RATP app to plan your journey.

Beyond the underground, subways, buses, and trams create a web through Paris, giving plenty of options to explore. Buses 21 and 73 provide a tour around the city. The five RER lines also weave through Paris, stretching into the suburbs. Additionally, Transilien is similar to RER but focuses on suburban connections, making all the banlieues easily accessible.

For a short visit to Paris, consider the Navigo Découverte or Navigo Easy pass, a flexible travel option with access to the city's extensive public transport network. The Navigo pass is a rechargeable contactless smart card that allows travel on buses, trams, and the metro within specified zones. You can load single-trip tickets, a carnet of ten trips, or day passes onto the card. Navigo pass is available at metro and RER stations.

Bar des Quais

And there are even more interesting ways to visit Paris. Cycling around the city, you can explore more in a shorter timeframe. Dedicated bike lanes along the Seine and throughout the city make cycling a valid option. Velib', the bike-sharing system, allows you to easily rent and return bikes at numerous locations. You can buy a 1-, 2- or 3-day rental pass on their website. Or use the shared one of the many shared e-bikes: just download their app and go.

A Seine River cruise gives a different perspective on the city and its landmarks. Daytime cruises provide a relaxed atmosphere, allowing you to see multiple monuments in a short time, while evening cruises offer breathtaking views as the city lights up.

If you have the time, there is a lot to discover just outside of Paris, and public transport allows you to take day trips. Consider nearby destinations like Versailles, Giverny, or a *château* for an experience beyond the city limits.

WHERE TO STAY

The People

thepeoplehostel.com

This hip hostel chain is planning to take over Europe. There currently are four Paris locations: Belleville (11th arr.), Marais (4th arr.), Nation (12th arr.) and Bercy (12th arr.). These upscale boutique hostels offer comfortable beds and modern amenities in shared or private rooms. The People hostels provide a quiet and safe stay, are clean and offer good value for money.

Mije Marais

12 Rue des Barres, 75004 Paris, mije.com

The Mije Marais hostel stands out as begin the best located, benefiting from easy access to bars, cafes, and attractions in the vibrant neighbourhood. The 17th-century building it's housed in gives it plenty of charm. While receiving positive reviews and offering a modest free breakfast, it lacks a kitchen and may be quieter than other hostels.

Le Regent Montmartre

37 Boulevard Marguerite de Rochechouart, 75009 Paris, leregent.com

Nestled just down the hill from the iconic Sacré Cœur, Le Regent Montmartre of Hiphophostels is one of Paris' most popular hostels. While it officially sits just outside of Montmartre, its proximity to the artistic neighbourhood is a huge draw. Because of its size and modern look, the hostel feels somewhat like a hotel, but the ambience is warm and lively.

Vintage Hostel Gare Du Nord

73 Rue de Dunkerque, 75009 Paris, vintage-hostel.com

Conveniently close to Paris' main station, you'll find Vintage Hostel Gare Du Nord. This Hiphophostel has a local, vibrant atmosphere with lively bars and restaurants at just a minute's walk. Unfortunately, the hostel doesn't offer a free breakfast, but they compensate with free Wi-Fi. It has nothing but positive reviews about its cleanliness and comfort.

Generator Paris

9-11 Place du Colonel Fabien, 75010 Paris, staygenerator.com

Generator Paris is a large, modern hostel with a hotel-like feel, comfortable beds, contemporary amenities, and high standards for cleanliness. Despite limited community vibes reported by some, the hostel has plenty of communal space. The hostel lacks a kitchen but has a restaurant and outdoor terrace. With stunning rooftop views, a chic bar, and a relaxed atmosphere, it's hands down the best hostel for solo travellers exploring Paris.

Peace & Love

245 Rue La Fayette, 75010 Paris, peaceandlovehostel.com

Peace & Love is a top backpacker's choice in Paris, known for its vibrant atmosphere and well-equipped kitchen. While it's not very modern, it offers a fantastic party vibe with an on-site bar and popular pub games. The hostel provides various room options, from private to large dorms, and is conveniently located near a metro station and the scenic Canal Saint-Martin.

Beau M

108 Rue Damrémont, 75018 Paris, beaumhostel.com

Beau M is one of Paris' most popular hostels and stands out for its stylish and modern interior. It offers both private and shared rooms, including dorms with up to twelve beds. Dorms are either mixed or female-only, providing a safe and welcoming space for female solo travellers.

Plug Inn

7 Rue Aristide Bruant, 75018 Paris, plug-inn.fr

Plug Inn Montmartre, a recent addition to the Paris hostel scene, has become one of the city's most popular. The boutique hostel has modern comforts, but it lacks extensive social spaces, making it less favourable for meeting fellow travellers. However, its charming Montmartre location makes it appealing, as well as the free towels, free breakfast, and free walking tours.

Caulaincourt

2 Square Caulaincourt, 75018 Paris, caulaincourt.com

Hiphophostels presents Caulaincourt, another centrally located hostel in the charming Montmartre area. Catering to backpackers, it offers Wi-Fi, hot water, maps, and a free French-style breakfast. They offer private, twin, and dorm rooms conveniently close to local attractions and a metro station. The hostel lacks luxury but provides all the essentials for a pleasant stay while exploring Paris.

St. Christopher's Inn Canal

159 Rue de Crimée, 75019 Paris, st-christophers.co.uk

A top pick for budget travellers in Paris, St. Christopher's Inn Canal is known for its good location, friendly staff, and cleanliness. An ideal place if you're looking for a lively atmosphere: the hostel features an on-site bar and club with drink discounts. It overlooks the canal and hosts regular social events. The hostel has a bit of a party reputation, but it provides under-bed lockers and privacy curtains, ensuring a good night's sleep.

The Social Hub La Défense

56 Rue Roque de Fillol, 92800 Puteaux, thesocialhub.co

The Social Hub in La Défense offers a unique blend of modern comfort and social connectivity. Located in the bustling business district, it serves as a hub for professionals and travellers alike. With modern amenities, a welcoming atmosphere and communal spaces, the hotel encourages social interaction and provides the perfect stay.

Mama Shelter

mamashelter.com

If you value privacy, a hostel might not be for you. Luckily, Paris also offers trendy affordable hotels. Exciting design, inclusivity, good food, and a playful atmosphere: Mama Shelter in a nutshell. Choose your stay at Mama Paris East or West. Even if you don't take shelter here, you must grab a bite at one of the restaurants or have a drink on the rooftop.

GOOD TO KNOW

French

French is the official language, and while many Parisians speak English, it's appreciated when you attempt basic French phrases. A simple *Bonjour* (Good day), *Au revoir* (Goodbye) or *Merci* (Thank you) goes a long way. After working hours, around 5 or 6pm, the French switch to *Bonsoir* (Good evening).

Opening hours

In Paris, many businesses are always open, but some have a set closing time. Before setting off, check opening times online to avoid closed doors. Please note that the Parisians celebrate their summer holidays in August, so smaller shops may be closed for the month.

Sights & museums
Many Parisian sights, like the Eiffel Tower and Arc de Triomphe, are open all day every day. Most museums are open 10 or 11am to 6 or 7pm, and some stay open to visitors one evening each week. Many are closed either on Mondays or Tuesdays.

Shops
Shops and businesses often close on Sundays and/or Mondays, while some are open all week. Most open around 10 or 11am on weekdays, while some will be closed until 12 or 2pm on Sundays. Closing time is almost always between 7 and 8pm. Smaller businesses may close for an extended lunch break between 12 and 2pm.

Markets
Opening times of local markets may vary. Most

set up for the weekend, while others take place one weekday. Markets mostly open early in the morning, around 7am, and close around lunchtime, even though some markets run all day. All markets and opening times are advertised on *paris.fr/marches.*

Paris is also famous for its many vintage markets. On Saturdays and Sundays, several flea markets can be found throughout the city. Some markets take place on Thursdays. Like other markets, most flea markets open early in the morning and close around 1 or 2pm. Locations and times change each week, so look them up in advance.

Eating habits

Parisians take their meals very seriously and the dining experience is an important part of French culture. You start the day with *petit déjeuner* (breakfast), usually a croissant or a baguette with butter and jam, and some coffee or tea. From 12 to 2pm, the French have their lunch break and they like to take their time for a large hot meal, or *déjeuner*. Parisians often go out for lunch, and many restaurants offer a *formule déjeuner*, which is a cost-effective lunch option with a starter and main, or main and dessert for €15-20.

Around 6pm, before dinner, it's time for the beloved *apéro*. This involves a drink (wine, vermouth, or a light cocktail) and bites like olives or cheese. Apéro is a time for relaxation and conversation before the main meal, which starts at 7.30pm at the earliest. A lot of bars offer Happy Hour around 6 to 8pm, with discounted drinks.

The French usually like their meat, but it is certainly possible to find good vegetarian and vegan options. Good to know: *végétarien(ne)* means vegetarian and *végétalien(ne)* means vegan in French, although the word *vegan* is used as well.

Where to eat?

In Paris there's a café, *bistrot* or *brasserie* on every street corner. So how do they compare?

Cafés are typical to Parisian culture, known for their outdoor seating and relaxed atmosphere. They primarily serve coffees and teas, and sometimes offer light meals, pastries, or snacks. They often feature sidewalk seating, making them a great place for people-watching and socialising.

A *bistrot* is a cosy, casual eatery known for its warm and friendly atmosphere. *Bistrots* typically offer a concise menu with traditional French comfort food, emphasising locally sourced and seasonal ingredients. Their décor is simple, with chalkboard menus and an informal setting.

Brasseries are larger than *Bistrots* and the atmosphere is often livelier. They offer menus with a variety of dishes, including seafood, meats, and regional specialties. Some *brasseries* are open late into the night.

Bouillons historically served affordable, hearty meals to the working class. Their menus feature simple, traditional French dishes at affordable prices. A bouillon usually has a straightforward, no-frills decor, and provides value for money.

Other restaurants in Paris vary widely and range from casual to fine dining. Restaurants can offer a diverse menu that may include regional specialties, international cuisine, or gourmet dishes. Their ambiance varies, from intimate settings to upscale and formal dining experiences.

If you want to immerse yourself in French culture, try some traditional dishes. As a starter, have some *œuf mayonnaise* (eggs with mayonnaise), *escargots* (snails) or *soupe à l'oignon* (onion soup with cheese). Classic main dishes include *coq au vin* (chicken in red wine), *bœuf bourguignon* (beef stew), *ratatouille* (vegetable stew) or *confit de canard* (slow-cooked duck). As a dessert, try *crème brûlée* (a rich custard, topped with a layer of hardened caramelised sugar), *tarte tatin* (an upside-down apple tart), *profiteroles* (choux pastry balls with a sweet filling), *pain perdu* (French toast with a creamy coating) or a *crêpe* (a thin French pancake with sweet or savoury toppings). If you want to fully adopt the French ways, have a cheese plate before dessert.

Service charge is included in restaurant bills, but it's customary to leave some change as a gesture of appreciation. Additionally, it's polite to greet the staff upon entering a restaurant and you must wait to be seated.

A few tips

Are you under 26 and an EU citizen? Most monuments and museums are free to visit. At other venues you receive a discount. Always take proof of ID!
The official currency in France is the euro. Credit cards are widely accepted, and you will be able to pay contactless with your debit card or smartphone. Bring some cash just in case, especially when you go to smaller businesses or markets.
Parisians tend to dress smartly. While casual attire is acceptable in most places, you might want to dress up a bit when dining out or visiting upscale venues. Entry to a club may be refused if you are not dressed accordingly.
If you plan to visit multiple

museums and monuments, the Paris Museum Pass saves time and money, allowing fast track access to many spaces.
Paris is generally safe, but be cautious of pickpockets, especially in crowded tourist areas. Always keep an eye on your belongings.

Check the weather forecast before your trip, as Paris experiences distinct seasons. Layers are advisable, and a compact umbrella can be handy, especially in spring and autumn.

WHEN TO TRAVEL

#PERFECT
HOTEL & HOSTEL

PARIS IN SPRING

In spring, Paris turns green, making it the perfect time to explore spots like Parc Monceau and Parc des Buttes-Chaumont. Check out the Eiffel Tower and Trocadéro to witness the beauty of cherry blossoms. Take a bike ride along the Seine and take in the lovely views that only springtime in Paris can offer. April brings not just blooming flowers but also the city's marathon, adding an athletic touch to the season.

As the sun warms the city, terraces and rooftops come back to life, offering perfect spots to grab a coffee or have a delicious meal. Chill in urban forest Bois de Boulogne, a peaceful getaway with draws like Jardin d'Acclimatation and Fondation Louis Vuitton. Bois de Vincennes is another beautiful green spot, with Château de Vincennes and a zoo.

Immerse yourself in the city's culture during Nuit Européenne des Musées and Nuit Blanche. Art comes alive, and the city becomes a canvas for creativity after dark. Fashion enthusiasts can catch a glimpse of the latest trends during Paris Fashion Week, an extravagant showcase that spills over from late spring into early summer.

Keep in mind that this is also the season for numerous holidays, from Easter to Ascension Day and Whitsun, to Labour Day on the 1st and Liberation Day on 8th May, for which some shops and restaurants close.

PARIS IN SUMMER

Summer in Paris kicks off in style on 21st June with Fête de la Musique, a musical event that fills the city with rhythm and melody. Live bands, DJs, and musicians can be found everywhere, from major squares and parks to impromptu street parties to which people bring their own music.

Spread your blanket by the Seine or Canal Saint-Martin for a picnic or drinks. The city also hosts Paris Plage, an annual event that transforms different spots along the Seine and Bassin de la Villette into makeshift beaches, providing a unique summer experience.

Celebrate diversity at Paris Pride at the end of June and on 14th July join the festivities for the national holiday. The day features a military parade known as Défilé, followed by evening fireworks at the Eiffel Tower. Don't miss Le Bal des Pompiers the night before, a lively firefighter's ball to kick off the celebrations.

Experience the magic of outdoor cinema at Parc de la Villette and take a stroll along La Coulée Verte, also known as la Promenade Plantée, a railway bridge turned into a park. Good to know: in August, Paris is relatively quiet, as many locals are on holiday, making it the perfect time to explore the city at a more relaxed pace.

DE MES
FRASQUES
JE FAIS
DES
FRESQU

PARIS IN AUTUMN

Autumn in Paris is a fantastic mix of lively events and cosy vibes that you won't want to miss. Enjoy the autumnal colours around the city. Places like Champ de Mars and Père Lachaise look stunning with the yellow and red leaves. Discover *Le mur des feuilles* on Rue Saint Vincent in Montmartre, covered in vibrant red leaves. Or take it easy in the Japanese garden at Albert Kahn.

Discover the city's hidden treasures during Journées du Patrimoine, the European Heritage Days, mid-September. Historic monuments, typically off-limits, open their doors, with a different theme each year. Just make sure to book in advance.

If you're into music and like a street party vibe, come to the Techno Parade. Picture yourself walking along a dozen floats from different radio stations, each blasting its unique techno style. The parade takes different routes through Paris, making it a different experience each year.

Experience Fête des Vendanges around Sacré-Cœur in Montmartre for a lively festival feel. Stalls from French winemakers, local food, and a vibrant atmosphere make it a must-visit spot. And get into the Halloween spirit by wandering famous cemeteries like Cimetière Père Lachaise, Cimetière Montparnasse, or Cimetière Montmartre.

In November, celebrate Beaujolais Nouveau on the third Thursday of the month, a perfect excuse to have some fresh and fruity wine. Embrace the cosy side of Paris on a rainy autumn day by wandering through its museums or covered passages, immersing yourself in art, history, and culture.

PARIS IN WINTER

Winter in Paris is like stepping into a festive fairy tale with the *illuminations de Noël* (Christmas lights). Champs Élysées is a glowing spectacle, and the festive decorations extend to Avenue Montaigne, Place Vendôme, and the amazing Christmas displays at Galeries Lafayette, La Samaritaine, Printemps Haussmann, Bon Marché, and BHV-Marais. The city dresses up perfectly to get into the Christmas spirit.

The holiday spirit is alive at the charming Christmas markets, each with its own unique flair. From Le Marché de Noël Alsacien (a French region in the east with German influences), to the magical Village de Noël de l'Hôtel de Ville, these markets offer a festive experience. Treat yourself with cheesy meals like *raclette* and cosy up at spots like Pain Vin Fromages or Les Fondus de la Raclette.

For a low-key escape that doesn't break the bank, catch a film in cinemas around Montparnasse. Classic gems like Christine 21 add a touch of nostalgia. Just make sure to choose VO (*Version Originale*) for an authentic film experience, rather than VF (*Version Française*).

Don't miss the glitz of Paris Fashion Week in January, bringing a dose of glamour to the city. Warm up in a local *bistrot* with a comforting hot chocolate or embrace the winter vibes with some ice skating.

LIFE IN PARIS

HISTORY

Origins of Paris

The area that is now Paris was initially inhabited by a Gallic tribe known as the Parisii, who established a settlement on the Île de la Cité around 250 BCE. In the 1st century BCE, the Romans conquered the area, establishing a thriving city they called Lutetia on the Left Bank of the Seine. The name comes from the Gallic word for marsh or swamp. Roman conquerors Latinized this Gallic name into Lutetia Parisiorum, emphasising its association with the local Gallic tribe, the Parisii. The choice of the name likely reflects the geography of the region, as Île de la Cité, the central island in the Seine where Lutetia was situated, was characterised by boggy areas. As the Roman Empire flourished, Lutetia evolved into an essential urban centre. In the 12th century, Paris became the capital of the Kingdom of France. This pivotal role marked the beginning of the city's ascent to cultural and political prominence. Through the mediaeval period, the Renaissance, and the Enlightenment, Paris retained its significance.

Enlightenment

The Enlightenment in Paris during the 18th century was a transformative intellectual and cultural movement that deeply influenced the city's landscape. As a hub of philosophical and scientific innovation, Paris became a beacon of rational thought, questioning traditional authority and promoting the values of reason, individual rights, and progress. The salons, such as those hosted by Madame Geoffrin and Madame de Pompadour, became intellectual forums where thinkers like Voltaire, Rousseau, and Diderot exchanged ideas that shaped the era's philosophical foundations. The *Encyclopédie*, edited by Diderot and d'Alembert, was a monumental work representing the Enlightenment's commitment to knowledge distribution. Parisian thinkers paved the way for secularism, scientific research, and questioning of established norms, laying the groundwork for societal transformation. The Enlightenment in Paris, marked by a spirit of intellectual curiosity and critical thinking, laid the foundation for the principles that would later shape modern Western thought.

Bastille Day and the French Revolution

Bastille Day, celebrated annually on 14th July, marks the historic storming of Bastille prison in 1789, a significant event that triggered the French Revolution. The Bastille, a symbol of royal oppression, became the central point for the fight for freedom and justice. The day is commemorated with festivities across France, including a military parade on Champs-Élysées and fireworks at the Eiffel Tower. Throughout France, citizens take part in celebrations, including fireworks, parties, and concerts, symbolising the ideals of the Revolution – liberty, equality, and fraternity. The French Revolution, lasting ten years from 1789 to 1799, reshaped the course of history by challenging the centuries-old monarchy and advocating for principles of liberty, equality, and fraternity. King Louis XVI and Queen Marie Antoinette symbolised the opulence and indifference of the monarchy, leading to widespread dissatisfaction. The revolution led to the abolishment of absolute monarchy and the First French

Republic was established in 1792. The revolution's course was complex and marked by internal conflicts, external threats, and the radical Reign of Terror led by the Jacobins, resulting in mass executions, including the guillotine deaths of Louis XVI and Marie Antoinette. Despite its complexity, the French Revolution left a lasting legacy, shaping political ideals and inspiring global movements for democracy and human rights. Napoleon Bonaparte's rise to power in 1799 marked the ending of this transformative period.

Arrondissements

The origin of the Paris *arrondissements* can be traced back to the administrative reforms that started during the French Revolution. In 1795, the revolutionary government reorganised Paris, dividing it into twelve districts, or *arrondissements*, to decentralise power. The goal was to simplify governance, enhance local representation, and eliminate traces of the royal regime. Each *arrondissement* became an independent administrative unit with its own mayor and council. Over time, the number of arrondissements grew, and eventually became the current twenty in 1860, under the guidance of Napoleon III and architect Georges-Eugène Haussmann. Haussmann's ambitious urban renewal projects, such as the creation of wide boulevards, also contributed to the modern layout of the *arrondissements*. The Paris *arrondissements* form a spiral pattern, resembling the structure of a snail shell. The twenty administrative districts are arranged in a clockwise manner radiating outward from the central point on Île de la Cité. The arrondissements also reflect the diverse character of Paris, and each district has its own unique charm, history, and cultural identity.

Banlieues

After World War II, rapid urbanisation led to the expansion of the city's suburbs, the *banlieues*. They offered affordable housing and accommodated the influx of immigrants. The *banlieues* evolved into diverse communities. In the second half of the 20th century, economic shifts resulted in deindustrialisation, which had a major impact on employment opportunities in these suburbs. By the late 20th and early 21st century, certain *banlieues* faced unemployment, poverty, and occasional social unrest. Factors such as a lack of investment in infrastructure, perceived discrimination, and issues related to integration contributed to tensions. The government launched initiatives to emphasise urban renewal, educational programs, and social integration efforts.

Expositions Universelles

Paris hosted two World's Fairs, in 1889 and 1900, each with a lasting impact on the city's identity. The 1889 Exposition Universelle celebrated the French Revolution's centennial and introduced the iconic Eiffel Tower to showcase both technological expertise and national pride. The tower became an enduring symbol of Paris. At the time, millions flocked to witness technological wonders and diverse cultural exhibits. In 1900, the city welcomed the world for another Exposition Universelle, emphasising cultural diversity, art, and scientific achievements. The fair, held in the beautiful Grand Palais and Petit Palais, showcased Art Nouveau designs and innovative inventions, and unveiled the new Paris Métro. The fairs

METRO

AVENUE DE
MONTSOURIS

not only transformed Paris into a global hub for innovation but also influenced perceptions of progress, leaving a mark on the city's cultural and architectural landscape.

Les Catacombes

Les Catacombes have a fascinating history that dates back to the late 18th century. Originally, these underground tunnels were limestone quarries, providing building materials for the city as it expanded. As Paris grew, so did the need for additional burial space, and in the late 18th century the crowded cemeteries became a threat to public health.

In response, the remains of over six million people were moved into the tunnels, a process which continued into the 19th century. The bones were arranged in an organised manner, creating morbid but intriguing patterns. Les Catacombes became a place of historical and cultural interest and opened to the public in the early 19th century. It still serves as a unique underground museum, giving visitors a glimpse into the city's history, burial practices, and architectural adaptation of underground spaces.

Moulin Rouge

In 1889, Joseph Oller and Charles Zidler, opened this now legendary cabaret. During the Belle Époque, the Moulin Rouge quickly became an icon of bohemian Parisian nightlife. Its extravagant shows, featuring can-can dancers, singers, and performers, often pushed the boundaries of modern entertainment. The red windmill on top of the building became a symbol for the Moulin Rouge, attracting visitors and artists from around the world. The cabaret survived two World Wars and continued to evolve with the times. It played a significant role in the cultural and artistic movements of the early 20th century. Today, the Moulin Rouge remains a vibrant cultural institution, synonymous with the spirit of Parisian festivity and the enduring allure of cabaret entertainment.

Student protests of 1968

The Paris student protests in 1968 marked a turning point in global history, reflecting a widespread desire for social and political change. They began as a series of demonstrations by university students against bureaucratic and authoritarian policies but quickly snowballed into a nationwide movement. The protesters, fuelled by unhappiness with the conservative establishment and inspired by anti-Vietnam War feelings, called for greater personal freedoms, educational reforms, and an end to societal constraints. The protests intensified in May 1968, reaching a climax in mass demonstrations and strikes that paralysed the country. The movement gained support from different parts of society, including labour unions. Workers joined the students in solidarity, leading to one of the largest general strikes in French history.
The protests had a profound impact on French society, causing political and cultural shifts. While the immediate political gains were limited, the events of May 1968 left an enduring legacy, influencing later social movements.

SIGHTSEEING

La Conciergerie & Sainte-Chapelle

2 Boulevard du Palais, 75001 Paris, paris-conciergerie.fr, 10 Boulevard du Palais, 75001 Paris, sainte-chapelle.fr

La Conciergerie on Île de la Cité was the residence of the kings of France but turned into a prison during the French Revolution. In 1793, Marie Antoinette was held here for over seventy days. Nowadays you can take an interactive tour that offers a glimpse into Paris' mediaeval history. Tour de l'Horloge houses the oldest clock of Paris. Next door, you'll find Sainte-Chapelle, built by King Louis IX to house the most prestigious relics of the Passion of Christ: The Crown of Thorns and a fragment of the True Cross. The queue takes a while, but the fifteen stunning stained-glass windows are worth the wait.

Église Saint-Eustache

2 Impasse Saint-Eustache, 75001 Paris, saint-eustache.org

In the heart of Les Halles, Église Saint-Eustache is the perfect mix of Renaissance and Gothic. Due to a lack of money, it took over a century to finish the church, which caused the transition of the architectural style. The exterior is beautiful, resembling Notre-Dame. Inside, the long pillars run to the high ceilings and light floods in through the stained-glass windows. Walk around to look at the magnificent organ and take in the exuberant decorations.

Galerie Vivienne

4 Rue des Petits Champs, 75002 Paris, galerie-vivienne.com

The city is full of old shopping arcades, inspired by Arab souks, but the most enchanting one must be Galerie Vivienne. Under the supervision of architect Haussmann, many glass-domed arcades disappeared, but Galerie Vivienne remained. The walk under its glass roof, past the elegant boutiques and over the mosaic floors will take you right back to the 19th century. Browse the books at Librairie Jousseaume or sit down for a *café* at *Bistrot* Vivienne.

Notre-Dame de Paris

6 Parvis Notre-Dame - Place Jean-Paul II, 75004 Paris, notredamedeparis.fr

Notre-Dame de Paris, a masterpiece of French Gothic architecture, holds a special place in the hearts of both Parisians and visitors. Unfortunately, since it was tragically damaged by a fire in 2019, people have only been able to appreciate its façade, as the cathedral has been closed for renovations. The reopening has been

↓ ARC DE TRIOMPHE

↓ SACRÉ-CŒUR

postponed many times and is now planned for December 2024. Until then, you can read all about the fire and reconstruction on the fences around Notre-Dame. The photos on the signs are quite impressive.

Grande Mosquée de Paris

2bis Place du Puits de l'Ermite, 75005 Paris, grandemosqueedeparis.fr

Tucked away in Quartier Latin, the Grande Mosquée de Paris is a hidden gem. The mosque was built as a monument to the Muslim victims of World War I. It is open to visitors and for a small fee you can discover this secret spot. Its intricate tilework, serene courtyard and gardens offer a unique escape. Afterwards, you can enjoy pastries and mint tea at the tearoom or have a traditional meal at the restaurant.

Panthéon

Place du Panthéon, 75005 Paris, paris-pantheon.fr

Built as a church, the Panthéon became a temple after the French Revolution. The Pantheon celebrates the values of the Republic, like braveness and union, and honours the important men and women of France. Politicians, writers, and philosophers such as Marie Curie, Victor Hugo and Voltaire are buried here. Spot all the great names while wandering through the crypt. Enjoy the architecture and decorations on the ground floor and walk the stairs to the dome for a panoramic view of Paris.

La Tour Eiffel

5 Avenue Anatole France, 75007 Paris, toureiffel.paris

Standing tall against the skyline, the Eiffel Tower is the most iconic symbol of Paris. When Gustave Eiffel designed it for the 1889 Exposition Universelle, the tower was met with mixed reactions. However, over time, it has become a famous sight, attracting millions of visitors each year. During the day, you can climb the tower and take in the breathtaking views of the city from the observation decks, or you can admire it from a distance at Champ-de-Mars or Place du Trocadéro. After sunset, the Eiffel Tower transforms into a glittering light show for five minutes once an hour. Prices depend on how far you go up and if you use the lift or stairs.

↓ LA TOUR EIFFEL

↓ PANTHÉON

Hôtel des Invalides

129 Rue de Grenelle, 75007 Paris, musee-armee.fr

When Hôtel des Invalides was built in 1670, it was originally a hospital for soldiers and a retirement home for war veterans. Now it houses Musée de l'Armée, showcasing France's military history. Other museums in the building are Musée des Plans et Reliefs and Musée de l'Ordre de la Libération. Or visit the Dôme des Invalides, where the tomb of Napoleon Bonaparte is a significant attraction. If you'll book a ticket for AURA Invalides at night, you'll witness an immersive lightshow in the dome.

Arc de Triomphe

Place Charles de Gaulle, 75008 Paris, paris-arc-de-triomphe.fr

At the western end of the Champs-Élysées, you'll find one of Paris' most impressive monuments. In 1806, Napoleon ordered the construction of the Arc de Triomphe after his victory at Austerlitz. It took thirty years to complete. You can still admire the arch and climb it for impressive views over the city. A tunnel located at Champs-Élysées will take you where you need to be; don't risk your life crossing the roundabout to get to the Arc. Tickets to climb to the top are sold at the same spot.

Opéra Garnier

Place de l'Opéra, 75009 Paris, operadeparis.fr

Palais Garnier (1875) is one of the world's most famous opera houses. You can take a tour of the building during the day or if you're lucky enough to get your hands on a ticket, attend a performance. Look up to see the ceiling painted by Marc Chagall. And prepare to be wowed by the grand staircase. The entrance alone is enough to warrant a visit. You will be able to explore the different floors and attached rooms.

Basilique du Sacré-Cœur

35 Rue du Chevalier de la Barre, 75018 Paris, sacre-coeur-montmartre.com

Although the history of this striking white presence causes some fuss among Parisians, the Basilique du Sacré-Cœur at the top of the hill of Montmartre is worth a visit. The basilica is named after the biblical Sacred Heart and was built to ask forgiveness for the cruelties of the Franco-Prussian War at the end of the 19th century. The interior is as stunning as the exterior, and is decorated with paintings, sculptures, and a large mosaic of Jesus. Dare to climb the steps for a panoramic view from the dome (at an extra cost), or just watch the city from the stairs where a lot of people gather for drinks and to watch street artists perform.

Cimetière du Père-Lachaise

16 Rue du Repos, 75020 Paris, pere-lachaise.com

Cimetière du Père-Lachaise is Paris' largest cemetery. The expressive tombs, small palaces and statues make it a cemetery like no other, and it's excellent for a peaceful stroll to contemplate and reflect on life. Père-Lachaise serves as the final resting place of countless famous people, attracting a lot of visitors. Wandering the cobblestone paths, you may see the graves of writers Oscar Wilde and Marcel Proust, musicians Jim Morrison and Édith Piaf, and many more.

ECOURS
EN CAS DE NOYADE OU ACCIDENT
DEMANDEZ
FLUVIALE: 47 07 17 17 ou 17
SAPEURS POMPIERS

MUSEUMS

Musée du Louvre

4 Place du Louvre, 75001 Paris, louvre.fr

The iconic Louvre acts as a time machine and you'll get lost in time and culture. The former palace of the kings of France, including Louis XIV, is the largest museum in the world, and more than 480,000 works cover almost 10,000 years of art history. The museum is divided into three wings: Richelieu, Sully, and Denon, where you'll find *Mona Lisa*, Egyptian artefacts and countless paintings and statues. Every corner reveals a new surprise. Entry is free for under 26s. The museum has different entrances, the main entrance under the famous glass Pyramid.

Musée des Arts Décoratifs

107 Rue de Rivoli, 75001 Paris, madparis.fr

Adjacent to the Louvre lies a beautiful museum with a mix of furniture, jewellery, fashion, and graphic design. Musée des Arts Décoratifs has an impressive permanent collection, but the temporary fashion and design exhibitions excite the Parisians most. The most inspiring designers and artists have displayed stunning fashion pieces at MAD.

Musée de l'Orangerie

Jardin des Tuileries, 75001 Paris, musee-orangerie.fr

Next door to Jeu de Paume (see page 59), you'll find a museum devoted to impressionist and post-impressionist art. The collection on the ground floor of Musée de l'Orangerie is well-worth the visit, but most visitors are here for one thing only: the breathtaking *Water Lilies* by Monet. The famous painting covers eight walls in two rooms, enabling you to appreciate the masterpiece from every angle.

Musée Carnavalet

23 Rue de Sévigné, 75003 Paris, carnavalet.paris.fr

Ever wondered how Paris was founded? And what happened during the French Revolution? In the heart of the city, you can learn all about its history at Musée Carnavalet. It is housed in two

↓ MUSÉE DU LOUVRE

↓ CENTRE POMPIDOU

↓ MUSÉE D'ORSAY

large 16th and 17th century mansions. After a four-year renovation, you can now (re)discover the rich collection in sixty rooms (yes ... the museum is huge). There is no doubt you will be impressed by the exhibition as well as the buildings and their rooms.

Centre Pompidou

Place Georges-Pompidou, 75004 Paris, centrepompidou.fr

Centre Pompidou isn't for the conservative: its inside-out design screams modernity. It hosts a playground of modern and contemporary art, showing masterpieces by Picasso, Duchamp, and other creative minds. The building not only houses the Museum of Modern Art with a permanent art collection and temporary exhibitions, but also contains a library, cinema, café, and restaurant. Take the escalators to the top floor for one of the best views over the city.

Musée d'Orsay

Esplanade Valéry Giscard d'Estaing, 75007 Paris, musee-orsay.fr

A former railway station turned art hotspot, that's Musée d'Orsay. The museum exhibits art from the late 19th and early 20th century, housing impressive works by impressionists such as Van Gogh and Monet. With paintings and statues from all over the world, Musée d'Orsay is one of the most interesting museums in Paris. Explore each floor and make your way up to catch a glimpse of the giant station clock that overlooks the Seine.

Jeu de Paume

1 Place de la Concorde, 75008 Paris, jeudepaume.org

This hidden gem for fans of cutting-edge visuals is nestled in Jardins des Tuileries. It was built as a tennis court but is now a hotspot for contemporary art. Since 2004, Jeu de Paume has shifted its focus to photography and video art. The museum's intimate setting and innovative exhibitions make it a dynamic cultural hub to immerse yourself in the landscape of modern visual arts.

Petit Palais

Avenue Winston Churchill, 75008 Paris, petitpalais.paris.fr

Petit Palais is not as small as it sounds. It is a true gem, housing the Musée des Beaux-Arts with a collection of amazing paintings and statues. Entrance to the permanent collection is free, but a fee is charged for temporary exhibitions. After you've admired the art, visit the hidden courtyard to have a drink at the café or to just enjoy the beautiful garden.

↓ MUSÉE DES ARTS DÉCORATIFS

Galerie Dior

11 Rue François 1er, 75008 Paris, galeriedior.com

Galerie Dior is a tribute to the history of the fashion house of Christian Dior. The gallery shows the evolution of Dior's designs, from its origin in 1947 to modern fashion, featuring carefully preserved haute couture pieces, sketches, and accessories. Each room with a unique ambiance, making the creations come to life. Take a leisurely stroll and revel in the

↓ CENTRE POMPIDOU

↓ PALAIS DE TOKYO

↓ MUSÉE DE LA VIE ROMANTIQUE

creativity. Just around the corner is Avenue Montaigne. After your visit to the Galerie, indulge in some window shopping at Chanel, Louis Vuitton, Balenciaga, and many more.

Musée de la Vie Romantique

16 Rue Chaptal, 75009 Paris, museevieromantique. paris.fr

A museum all about the Romantic era, filled with love stories, dreamy paintings, and that warm fuzzy feeling. Can you picture it? Musée de la Vie Romantique is in a charming spot and feels like stepping into a Jane Austen novel, but with more art. After touring the rooms of the cosy mansion, take a seat in the beautiful rose garden and have a cup of tea at Rose Bakery.

Musée Guimet

6 Place d'Iéna, 75116 Paris, guimet.fr

Musée Guimet is the Asian tour you never knew you needed. From ancient wonders to modern masterpieces, it's a crash course in Asian art. Each exhibit is like a colourful page from a cultural comic book, inviting you to soak in the beauty and uniqueness of various traditions. From ancient artefact to contemporary art, Guimet has it all, making this a fun and enlightening visit for anyone curious about Asian artistic culture.

Palais de Tokyo

13 Avenue du Président Wilson, 75116 Paris, palaisdetokyo.com

Palais de Tokyo is the rebellious teenager of Paris' art scene. In 2012 it became Europe's largest contemporary art centre – and it doesn't play by the rules. The exhibitions feel like a visual rollercoaster, pushing the boundaries of what you thought art could be. Palais de Tokyo lets you meet the creators of the future.

STREET ART

Space Invaders

space-invaders.com

Since the late 1990s, the French artist Invader has placed mosaic tiles in the shape of Space Invader characters on buildings across Paris. The pixelated invaders from the classic video game form an iconic and playful representation of contemporary street art, blending nostalgia with a modern urban twist. You can find more than 1,500 of them scattered throughout Paris, including an enormous one at Fontaine Stravinsky by Centre Pompidou.

Jef Aérosol

jefaerosol.com

Another street art piece at Fontaine Stravinksy is *Chuuuttt!!!* by Jef Aérosol. His work, often featuring iconic figures and celebrities, decorates the city's walls, drawing attention with bold colours and impressive detailing. You can find his murals in Le Marais, Belleville, and Canal Saint-Martin. And you can also spot some of his gems in the 13th and 20th districts.

Miss.Tic

missticinparis.com

Miss.Tic, an iconic figure in Parisian street art, brings a unique voice to the city's visual landscape. Her distinctive black-and-white stencils feature empowering messages and captivating female figures, leaving a trail of feminist commentary. Scattered across Paris,

Miss.Tic's art transforms ordinary walls into poignant statements, inviting viewers to ponder the meeting point of art and feminism. Despite her passing in 2022, a lot of her work can still be found, especially in Butte-aux-Cailles.

Butte-aux-Cailles

Butte-aux-Cailles, 75013 Paris

Butte-aux-Cailles is a haven for street art enthusiasts. Its narrow streets and charming façades serve as an urban canvas for countless vibrant artworks. From murals to stencils, the area shows a diverse collection of street art, reflecting a dynamic cultural scene. Butte-aux-Cailles immerses you into the ever-evolving world of urban art in Paris.

↓ MUR DES JE T'AIME

Spot 13

47 Allée Paris-Ivry, 75013 Paris, spot13paris.com

Street art continues to weave its canvas in the 13th arrondissement, much to our delight. Just below the Lavo//matik gallery, Spot 13 offers an incredible open-air canvas, and they regularly invite new street artists to leave their artistic mark. A must-visit.

Boulevard Vincent Auriol

Boulevard Vincent Auriol, 75013 Paris

Boulevard Vincent Auriol, also in the 13th arrondissement, serves as a vibrant urban art gallery. Alongside the boulevard, you'll find huge murals and graffiti on the sides of buildings, including works from famous street artists such as Seth, D*Face and Shepard Fairey.

Keith Haring

149 Rue de Sèvres, 75015 Paris

Keith Haring created a work of art called *Tower*, which is 27 metres tall and 13 metres wide. It stands as a totem in the heart of the new garden of the Necker-Enfants Malades Hospital. This monumental work, a true symbol of life, hope and joy, was designed by the artist to 'entertain sick children now and in the future'.

Mur des je t'aime

Square Jehan Rictus, Place des Abbesses, 75018 Paris, lesjetaime.com

A calligrapher collected over three hundred ways to say *I love you* and collaborated with an artist to engrave these on lava stone tiles: *Le Mur des je t'aime*. This Wall of Love, consisting of 612 tiles, can be found in Montmartre. It's dedicated to language and celebrates the universality of love, making it a romantic spot to visit with your loved one. Or just a really cool photo spot. What languages do you recognise?

Canal de l'Ourcq

Canal de l'Ourcq, 75019 Paris

'The Parisian Brooklyn', some like to call the Canal de l'Ourcq neighbourhoods from the 19th arrondissement to Pantin. Originally supplying drinking water, the canal has evolved into a vital hub for Parisians. It's a perfect spot for a picnic, a nightlife destination, and a thriving artistic centre with an abundance of amazing street art, including some of activist artist dAcRuZ.

Belleville

Belleville, 75020 Paris

Belleville is a giant art playground. The streets are alive with colour and creativity, thanks to local as well as global street artists. Everywhere you look, a mural is telling a story, or a funky stencil is making a statement. This neighbourhood, known for its bohemian spirit, embraces street art as a powerful form of expression, creating an urban landscape where creativity knows no bounds.

CINEMA

Whether you're into classic films or the latest releases, Paris has it all. From charming historic venues to modern cinemas, the city's film scene is diverse. Good to know, in France, many films are still dubbed. If that's not your bag, avoid movies in VF (Version Française). Instead, see the VO, VOST or VOSTFR (Version Originale Sous-Titrée en Français), the original version with French subtitles. Grab your popcorn and enjoy!

mk2

mk2.com

At various locations, mk2 brings a modern twist to your movie outings. Whether you're into indie flicks or mainstream hits, mk2 promises a cinematic journey filled with diversity and excitement.

Cinéma du Panthéon

13 Rue Victor Cousin, 75005 Paris, cinemadupantheon.fr

Step back in time at Cinéma du Panthéon. One of Paris' oldest cinemas invites you to enjoy films in atmospheric surroundings steeped in history. Visiting on a weekday? Go for a drink at Le Salon, a space curated by the iconic Catherine Deneuve.

Christine 21

4 Rue Christine, 75006 Paris, pariscinemaclub.com/christine-cinema-club

Immerse yourself in cinematic wonders at Christine 21, a spot that fuses film with artistic vibes. It's your ticket to a unique cinematic experience, Parisian style.

Lucernaire

53 Rue Notre-Dame des Champs, 75006 Paris, lucernaire.fr

Tucked in the cosy corners of the 6th arrondissement, Lucernaire is your go-to spot for cinematic adventures. Feel the artistic vibe as you explore a mix of films and cultural happenings, adding a touch of bohemian flair to your movie nights.

La Cinémathèque française

51 Rue de Bercy, 75012 Paris, cinematheque.fr

Head to the 12th arrondissement for a rendez-vous with cinematic history at La Cinémathèque française. From classics to contemporary gems, this spot is a treasure trove for movie buffs seeking a nostalgic yet vibrant experience.

Studio 28

10 Rue Tholozé, 75018 Paris, cinema-studio28.fr

Uncover the charm of Montmartre at Studio 28, a cinema that echoes the late 19th century. Once a sanctuary for artistic legends like Jean Cocteau and André Breton, it invites you to bask in history while enjoying cinematic delights. Don't forget to chill on the patio, a perfect spot on sunny days.

Major cinemas: UGC, Gaumont, Pathé

uge.fr
gaumont.com
pathe.fr

For a more mainstream cinema fix, hit up UGC, Gaumont, or Pathé. These cinema giants offer a mix of big-screen thrills and arthouse wonders, catering to every taste. Staying in Paris for longer? The cinema chains offer passes for unlimited movies for only a small fee per month.

FESTIVALS

Cercle

insta @cerclemusic

Not a traditional festival: Cercle organises electronic music events at unique and iconic locations, broadcasting live DJ sets online. At various locations, check their Instagram. Sells out quickly!

Fête de la Musique

fetedelamusique.culture.gouv.fr

Held annually on 21st June, this city-wide music celebration features free performances of various genres across Parisian streets, parks, and venues.

Festival Paris L'Été

parislete.fr

A summer festival offering a range of cultural events, including theatre, dance, music, and visual arts, at different locations throughout the city. Three weeks in July.

We Love Green

Bois de Vincennes, 75012 Paris, welovegreen.fr

An eco-friendly music festival, three days in early June, combining live music with a focus on environmental sustainability, attracting renowned artists and a green-conscious audience.

Solidays

2 Route des Tribunes, 75016 Paris, solidays.org

Music festival with a social cause, raising awareness and funds to combat HIV/AIDS, featuring a mix of international and local artists. Three days in June, at Hippodrome de Longchamp.

L'Été du Canal

Canal de l'Ourcq, 75019 Paris, lavillette.com

A summer festival along the Canal de l'Ourcq. Concerts, outdoor cinema, boat rides, and various cultural activities. It lasts from early July to mid-August. More information on the website, just look for this event.

Marvellous Island

Route de Lagny, 77200 Torcy, marvellous-island.fr

An electronic music festival that takes place on an island near Paris for two days in May. It offers an immersive experience with multiple stages and artistic performances.

Rock en Seine

Parc de Saint-Cloud, 92210 Saint-Cloud, rockenseine.com

One of the major French rock festivals, held in the Domaine National de Saint-Cloud, with rock, indie, and alternative music acts. Three days in August; buy a day pass or a ticket for the duration.

The Peacock Society Festival

Chemin des Bœufs, 94000 Choisy-le-Roi, peacocksociety.fr

Another electronic music festival, known for its cutting-edge line-up and vibrant atmosphere, held at Parc Floral de Paris, for two days in July.

La Plage de Glazart

7 Avenue de la Porte de la Villette, 75019 Paris, glazart.com/laplage

An open-air venue offering beach vibes, live music, and DJ sets: a unique summer experience in the heart of the city. Every weekend from June to September.

Cinéma en plein air La Villette

211 Avenue Jean Jaurès, 75019 Paris, lavillette.com

An outdoor film festival at Parc de la Villette, offering cinema under the stars. Four weeks during the summer months.

TOURS

Street art & feminism tour

feministsinthecity.com/paris

Street art tour in the old communist neighbourhood Butte-aux-Cailles. Discover the history of this neighbourhood, the movement for gender equality, and that of feminist street artists. Chances are you will see artists at work. Feminists in the City offer more feminism related tours.

Free walking tours

freewalkingtour.com/paris

Walking tours with proper storytelling. Explore various neighbourhoods with different tour options, from historic Paris to Quartier Latin. Pay what you can.

Street art tour

streetarttourparis.com

Take street art tours in areas like Belleville and Montmartre. Or explore tours in the western parts of Paris, offering a glimpse into neighbourhoods with captivating street art.

Haunted Paris tour

parisbyfoot.com/tour-item/haunted-tour

On the Haunted tour of Paris, you will discover the dark side of the city rarely seen even by Parisians. Many ghost stories, including the spooky story of Notre-Dame Cathedral.

Historical Crimes Walking Tour

book via getyourguide.com

Take an exciting walking tour to learn about shady dealings and other crimes that happened on the streets of Paris. Visit famous crime scenes and other spots. The tour is in French.

Holland bikes

locations.hollandbikes.com

A fun way to explore the city: enjoy the beautiful surroundings while comfortably riding a Dutch city bike, you'll cover a lot more ground than on foot. From a Highlights tour to a Secrets tour.

THINGS TO DO

La Petite Ceinture

petiteceinture.org

La Petite Ceinture, a repurposed abandoned railway line encircling Paris, offers a unique perspective off the beaten track. You can access Petite Ceinture at different locations.

59 Rivoli

59 Rue de Rivoli, 75001 Paris, 59rivoli.org

In a former squat, thirty artists exhibit their work, rotating periodically. Wander the six floors exploring the studios of various artists, each with their own style.

Marché des Enfants Rouges

39 Rue de Bretagne, 75003 Paris

Paris' oldest covered market, Marché des Enfants Rouges, dates back to the 17th century. Offering a diverse range of fresh produce and international cuisines: a food lover's dream.

Pottery and ceramics

bigbandpoterie.com ceramicafe-genevieve.fr

Get into pottery at Big Band Poterie, a former jazz café that now offers pottery classes with live jazz performances. Or take part in a work-shop at Ceramicafé Geneviève, the first ceramic café in Paris.

Bouldering

26bis Rue de Saint-Pétersbourg, 75008 Paris, climbingdistrict.com

At Climbing District, you can enjoy bouldering without needing a membership. The location near Gare Saint Lazare is very special, as it's based in an old chapel.

Escape rooms

17 Rue de la Pierre Levée, 75011 Paris, gamescape.fr

Escape rooms have become very popular in Paris. Enjoy thrilling scenarios, solving puzzles, and complete missions within creatively designed rooms. Gamescape offers escape rooms in English.

Les Catacombes

1 Avenue du Colonel Henri Rol-Tanguy, 75014 Paris, catacombes.paris.fr

Les Catacombes provide an historical experience like no other: an underground cemetery holding the remains of millions of Parisians. Explore the narrow tunnels covered in neatly arranged bones and skulls.

1 = 2€
3 = 5€
LES CATHARES EN OCCITANIE
La Fayette

FAMOUS PEOPLE (AND ONE CAT)

Josephine Baker

Arriving from America, Josephine Baker, the mesmerising singer, dancer, and civil rights activist, brought her thrilling performances to the stages of Paris. She amazed with her signature banana skirt and Charleston moves, becoming a sensation in the Roaring Twenties. Baker's captivating allure extended beyond entertainment: during World War II, she played a vital role in the French Resistance. Her legacy endures as a symbol of both artistic innovation as well as unwavering commitment to justice.

Simone de Beauvoir

As a pioneering philosopher, writer, and feminist, Simone de Beauvoir challenged the norms of society and became a key figure in existentialist thought in the 20th century. Her groundbreaking work *The Second Sex* questioned the role of women in society, sparking conversation about feminism and gender equality. A fearless advocate for women's rights and individual freedom, De Beauvoir's legacy continues to inspire generations of thinkers and activists worldwide.

Jane Birkin

Actress, singer, model, activist, style icon and inspiration for Hermès' famed Birkin bag. Jane Birkin lived a tumultuous life in the spotlight, for which her own delicate and intimate *chansons* provided the soundtrack. She left her native London for a role in the French movie *Slogan* (1969) and never left Paris again. The

1960's and 1970's it-girl had a timeless wardrobe, which is still seen as the blueprint for the Parisian dress sense today – maybe except for her love of mini skirts and dresses.

Marie Curie

To say that Maria Salomea Skłodowska-Curie was a remarkable woman is an understatement. At 24, the Polish-born scientist moved to Paris in 1891 to study mathematics, physics, and chemistry at the University of Paris. She went on to become its first female professor in 1906, the first woman to win the Nobel Prize for her research on radioactivity and the only person to date to be awarded the Nobel Prize in two sciences.

Dalida

The enchanting singer Dalida added a touch of glamour to Parisian nightlife with her captivating performances. Born in Egypt, she found a second home in the vibrant art scene of the French capital. Dalida's soulful voice brought timeless classics like *Bambino* and *Parole Parole*. She became a symbol of elegance and grace for audiences worldwide. Despite personal struggles, her songs continue to be celebrated, making her an icon in the city's musical history.

Daft Punk

The revolutionary French electronic music duo Daft Punk emerged from Paris. Their futuristic beats and iconic helmets revolutionised the global music scene with hits like *Get Lucky* and *Around the World*. Beyond their worldwide success, the duo significantly influenced Parisian nightlife, contributing to the city's dynamic creative energy. Known for their mysterious public identity, Daft Punk's unique approach reflects the mystique and allure of Paris, making them both global icons and local heroes.

Choupette Lagerfeld

Blue eyes, white fur ... it's not difficult to see why she was the (feline) muse of late fashion designer Karl Lagerfeld. Gifted to him in 2011, Choupette took the fashion world by storm and has since met and inspired many influential people, as the 2023 Met Gala made clear. The Birman moved in with her former nanny after Lagerfeld's death and still lives a luxurious life in her Paris apartment, which she documents on her very own Instagram page *@choupetteofficiel*.

Kylian Mbappé

Kylian Mbappé, the French football star, is known for his incredible speed and skill on the field. Born in 1998 in the Parisian suburb Bondy, he quickly made a name for himself at Paris Saint-Germain. Mbappé's remarkable talent, including his lightning-fast pace and precision in front of goal, helped the French national team win the FIFA World Cup in 2018. Off the field, he's admired for his humility, making him a favourite with fans worldwide.

Édith Piaf

The 'Little Sparrow' of French chanson left an emotional imprint on Paris with her soulful voice. Her timeless songs, like *La Vie en Rose*, capture the essence of love, heartbreak, and the spirit of the city. Rising from a chaotic background, Édith Piaf's emotional performances reflected her life's highs and lows. With a career that lasted decades, she became a symbol of French music, leaving a legacy that continues to resonate, making her a beloved figure at the heart of Parisian culture.

Pablo Picasso

One of the greatest artists of the 20th century spent most of his life in Paris. Dwelling in and around Montparnasse and Montmartre, where many other artists lived and worked, he got in touch with various art movements and styles that shaped his extensive repertoire. He painted *Guernica* (1937), an important anti-war portrayal, in his atelier on 7 Rue des Grands-Augustins. More infamously, he was a suspect in the 1911 heist of Leonardo da Vinci's *Mona Lisa* from the Louvre.

Voltaire

Voltaire, the Enlightenment philosopher, used his pen as a powerful weapon against injustice. His house became a hotspot for intellectual discussion, contributing to the city's reputation as a centre of enlightenment. His works, including *Candide*, challenged traditional norms and supported reason. Voltaire's influence extended beyond literature, sparking conversations about freedom and tolerance. His thought-provoking ideas shaped the Enlightenment era, solidifying his position as a pivotal figure in the landscape of Western philosophy.

Oscar Wilde

The witty Irish playwright and poet found his muse in the intellectual circles of Paris. Oscar Wilde was famous for his sharp wit and unconventional lifestyle. His residence became a hub for artistic discussions, adding a touch of eccentricity to Parisian culture. Wilde's important literary works, including *The Picture of Dorian Gray*, as well as his plays continue to captivate audiences, making him a timeless figure in both literature and Parisian history.

FILMS AND SERIES IN & ABOUT PARIS

Paris, je t'aime (2006)

This anthology takes you on a journey around Paris from the comforts of your sofa. Each of the eighteen short films takes place in a different *arrondissement* and shows the many ways in which love can be revealed, expressed, and felt. These heart-wrenching, comedic and sometimes outright bizarre vignettes that compose *Paris, je t'aime* couldn't be told better elsewhere, as the stunning backdrop of the city is a main character in and of itself.

120 Battements Par Minute (120 Beats Per Minute, 2017)

Set during the height of the global AIDS epidemic in the early 1990s, *120 Beats Per Minute* tells the story of the Paris division of ACT UP and its members. Whilst the group publicly protests the French government and pharmaceutical companies for their lack of action against HIV and AIDS, the activists each have their own battles to face. A poignant tale about the extension of the overarching political climate into the personal sphere, the Parisian queer community and love – in sickness and in health.

Midnight in Paris (2011)

Many writers and artists have found their muse in the city of Paris – and so has Woody Allen, it seems. His *Midnight in Paris* follows a miserable writer and his wife as they embark on a holiday to the French capital. When he takes a midnight stroll, he suddenly finds himself transported to the 1920s, and in the company of literary legends such as Zelda Fitzgerald and Ernest

Hemingway. This film is a feast for lovers of romantic fantasy, time travel and the arts.

Les Intouchables (The Intouchables, 2017)

Wealthy aristocrat and quadriplegic Philippe needs a caregiver; troubled and unambitious Driss just needs a signature to keep receiving his social benefits. But when Driss gives the job a try, a previously unseen side of him comes to the surface and a remarkable friendship is formed. Scenes that feature Philippe's impressive home in *The Intouchables* were filmed at Hôtel d'Avaray (85 Rue de Grenelle), the private residence of the Dutch ambassador.

Le Fabuleux Destin D'Amélie Poulain (Amélie, 2001)

When twenty-three-year-old Amélie moves to Paris to become a waitress, she finds a small treasure in her flat. Determined to find its owner (and succeeding), Amélie starts to live a life focused on helping others. But who helps Amélie to live the life she has always wanted for herself? *Le Fabuleux Destin D'Amélie Poulain* is a romantic comedy that paints a beautiful picture of Montmartre. The café where Amélie works, Café des 2 Moulins, can be found at 15 Rue Lepic.

The Eddy (miniseries, 2020)

Every city has its underbelly and so does Paris. When a musician travels from New York to Paris to run *The Eddy*, a struggling club and jazz band of the same name, he has to navigate the gritty waters of the city in order to keep the club open and the band swinging. The cast consists of musicians-as-actors rather than actors-as-musicians, so expect some jazzy tunes and captivating performances.

Before Sunset (2004)

After Jesse and Céline part ways in Vienna in *Before Sunrise* (1995), Jesse, inspired by their time together, proceeds to write a best-selling novel. During his book presentation at Shakespeare and Company – you probably know the one – he spots Céline in the crowd. In the hour before his flight back to the United States, the two go for a walk around Paris, engaging in personal conversations and rekindling their romantic fondness for each other. With much talking, walking and not much else, *Before Sunset* is a real-time film best suited for those who don't mind a slow burn.

Les Quatre Cents Coups (The 400 Blows, 1959)

Growing up in Paris, in the care of his laissez-faire mother and her absent husband, fourteen-year-old Antoine is a troublemaker - and misunderstood. When he is expelled from school, he starts engaging in petty crime and is ultimately admitted to a juvenile centre. The character study is realistic, thought-provoking and profound, and the Paris that is portrayed in *The 400 Blows* isn't the Paris you usually see in films. Cinephiles will appreciate the French New Wave characteristics in this picture.

Ratatouille (2007)

If a rat can become France's best chef, what's stopping you from following your dreams? In *Ratatouille*, Remy the rat and his rat family and rat friends live in an old lady's attic in Paris. But when they get discovered and evicted, Remy decides to follow his little nose to the restaurant of Auguste Gusteau. There, he helps binman Linguini to become a fine cook and, eventually, Remy himself becomes the star of Gusteau's kitchen. This wholesome animation will definitely make you crave ratatouille, so you might want to put it on your culinary bucket list for Paris.

Dix Pour Cent (Call My Agent! 2015-2020)

Client management isn't always easy – the agents in *Call My Agent!* know all about it. Every episode of this sophisticated comedy series features a French actor or actress playing themselves, as well as a recurring cast of endearing characters. The French humour, the satirical representation of the film industry and the fast-paced dialogue make this a particularly bingeable watch.

Taken (2008)

The premise of *Taken* is simple: Brian, former CIA officer, has 96 hours to find his precious daughter Kim, who has been kidnapped during a girl's trip to Paris. Torture, murder, high-speed chases – this action thriller has it all. It's an intense film, so sit back, buckle up and follow Brian's rampage through Paris as he does everything in his power to get his daughter back.

Le Bazar de la Charité (The Bonfire of Destiny, miniseries 2019)

In 1897, a large fire broke out in the Bazar de la Charité, killing 126 people – mostly aristocratic women selling artworks for charity. *Le Bazar de la Charité* is based on this real-life event and follows three women who survived the blaze whilst they navigate its tumultuous aftermath and the impact it has had on their lives.

BOOKS IN & ABOUT PARIS

A Tale of Two Cities – Charles Dickens

'It was the best of times, it was the worst of times'. A true classic with one of the most recognisable opening sentences, *A Tale of Two Cities* is set in London and Paris before and during the tumultuous French Revolution and the Reign of Terror. Expect a captivating read that covers important societal themes, as well as comedic padding and a cast of interesting, fleshed-out characters.

The Loveliest Chocolate Shop in Paris – Jenny Colgan

For lovers of cosy, romantic comedies (and chocolate, of course). Fluffy yet thought-provoking, *The Loveliest Chocolate Shop in Paris* makes your heart melt, and your tastebuds yearn. While Claire reflects on a sweltering summer in Paris in the 1970s, Anna has yet to make a life for herself in the city. Bonus points for the delicious recipes at the end of the book.

Paris Tales – Helen Constantine

Written by some of France's most inspiring authors past and present, *Paris Tales* take you to and through the various neighbourhoods of the city and their eccentric inhabitants. Whether you've already been, whether you're currently there or whether you're planning for a trip: this collection of short stories will transport you to the good, the bad, and the dirty parts of the city.

A Moveable Feast – Ernest Hemingway

Ernest Hemingway, well-known American author and winner of the Nobel Prize in Literature in 1954, once was a struggling writer and journalist in 1920s Paris. *A Moveable Feast* is his personal account of his time in the city, where he simultaneously experiences plenty of hardships and true *joie de vivre*. Some of the cafés and bars he mentions, such as La Closerie des Lilas, can still be visited today.

L'Elegance du herrison (The elegance of the Hedgehog) – Muriel Barbery

On 7 Rue de Grenelle, one of the most sophisticated streets of Paris, a woman and a girl live alongside one another, not realising how much they have in common. The moving story of Renée, concierge of the apartment building and twelve-year-old inhabitant Paloma, both exceptionally bright and talented, will have you reflect on stereotypes, class consciousness and compassion. *The Elegance of the Hedgehog* sold over two million copies in France and became an instant modern classic.

How Paris Became Paris: The Invention of the Modern City – Joan DeJean

Planning to walk your way through Paris, or are you hopping aboard the metro to take you from Pont Neuf to Île Saint-Louis? Whichever you choose, don't take the boulevards, bridges, sidewalks, streetlights, and public transport for granted. *How Paris Became Paris: The Invention of the Modern City* offers a compelling deep dive into the transformation of Paris from an urban mess in the 16th century to a liveable city in the 18th century.

Das Parfum (Perfume: The Story of a Murderer) – Patrick Süskind

Paris and perfume will always be connected – through Chanel No. 5 and the novel by Patrick Süskind. In *Perfume: The Story of a*

Murderer, we follow Paris-born Jean-Baptiste Grenouille, who has been blessed (or cursed?) with an exceptional sense of smell. What ensues is a bizarre tale about perfume-making, blinding passion and – indeed – murder.

The Paris Library – Janet Skeslien Charles

During World War II, the American Library in Paris never closed its doors on anyone, despite German interference and threats. Partly because of its courageous librarians that Janet Skeslien Charles gave the spotlight, the library is still thriving. *The Paris Library*, a historical fiction novel based on real-life events, tells the story of how librarian Odilie became part of the Resistance and how her books brought hope, connection, and bravery even in the darkest of times.

Le fantôme de l'Opera (The Phantom of the Opera) – Gaston Leroux

When Gaston Leroux worked as a journalist in Paris, a fatal accident occurred at Opéra Garnier. Amidst rumours that the building was haunted, a fire in the roof caused a chandelier to crash into the audience. And *The Phantom of the Opera* was born. When soprano Christine and her childhood lover Raoul renew their romance, jealousy drives the Phantom to haunt the opera until he gets what he desires most. Gothic horror at its finest!

FUN FACTS

Stop!

Nowadays, it will be impossible to find a stop sign in Paris. There used to be one in the city, but it was removed in 2016. Other traffic signs usually indicate prohibitions. Traffic is mainly regulated by traffic lights and the rule that traffic from the right always has priority.

Snail shell

Why is the numbering of *arrondissements* arranged like a snail shell? Initially, Paris had twelve arrondissements, numbered from left to right and from bottom to top, with 10, 11, and 12 below the river. With Haussmann's renovations, Paris expanded to twenty arrondissements, but the wealthy people in Passy (to the west) disagreed to become the 13th arrondissement. Their issue wasn't with the 'unlucky' association with the number, but with the fact that unmarried couples living together were said to be married in the (then non-existent) 13th arrondissement. The mayor of Passy proposed numbering the arrondissements in a spiral, making it the 16th.

Paris Syndrome

Paris Syndrome is a psychological condition primarily affecting Japanese tourists visiting Paris. These tourists experience disappointment when their romantic expectations of Paris don't match reality. The syndrome is attributed to a combination of culture shock, language barriers, and fatigue, characterised by hallucinations, paranoia, and depression, often caused by an extreme form of cultural disillusionment.

City of Light

Paris was the first city with streetlights, but 'City of Light' refers to the Enlightenment period rather than lights. However, light does play an important role in Paris. The Eiffel Tower, for instance, is beautifully illuminated in the evening with sparkling lights every hour for five minutes. The Eiffel Tower's lighting is even copyrighted.

↓ PONT NEUF

↓ PONT ALEXANDRE III

Pont Neuf

Le Pont Neuf, the bridge connecting the left and right banks and Île de la Cité, translates to the 'New Bridge', but it's the oldest bridge in the city, or at least the oldest surviving one.

Haussmann Buildings' Architecture

Haussmann buildings typically feature high-ceilinged ground floors for shops, a first floor (mezzanine) for storage or housing, a noble second floor with balconies, and subsequent floors with varying designs, including balconies and rooms for maids.

Statues of Liberty

The Statue of Liberty was made by Auguste Bartholdi, in Gustave Eiffel's workshop in the 17th arrondissement. It was a gift from France to the USA. There are five smaller replicas in Paris: on Île aux Cygnes, in Jardin du Luxembourg, at Musée d'Orsay, at Musée des Arts-et-Métiers, and you can find a replica of the Flame of Liberty at Pont de l'Alma. Since the tragic death of Princess Diana in 1997, this golden flame symbolises mourning.

Guillotine

The guillotine was introduced as a method of execution in 1792, during the French Revolution. It became a symbol of the Reign of Terror, used to execute thousands of people, including King Louis XVI and Queen Marie Antoinette. Although you might think of the guillotine as something from the distant past, France used it until 1977. You can still find traces of one of them in the road's surface on the corner of Rue de la Croix-Faubin and Rue de la Rouquette.

Baguette

It wouldn't be a cliché if it weren't true: baguettes are deeply rooted in French culinary culture. You can recognise the Frenchman in the bakery by whether he wants his baguette *bien cuite* (well-baked) or *pas trop cuite* (not too baked). A piece of baguette with salted butter is pure enjoyment for the French. An official law, known as the 'Decree Concerning the Characteristics of Bread', mandates that traditional French baguettes can only contain four ingredients: wheat flour, water, salt, and yeast or leavening agent.

Louvre

With nearly 8 million visitors, 30,000 a day, the Louvre is the most visited museum in the world, with the largest art collection. Visitors can view about 35,000 artworks, with many more in storage. They say that it would take up to one hundred days to see all the art in the Louvre. The value of the Louvre Museum and all its contents is estimated to be at least 40 billion euros.

PHOTO SPOTS

Colonnes de Buren

Galerie de la Cour d'Honneur, 2 Rue de Montpensier, 75001 Paris

In the Palais-Royal courtyard, Colonnes de Buren is a modern art installation with striped columns, creating a visually intriguing setting. The modern art combined with the historic building in the background offers an interesting contrast for your picture and reveals Paris' talent for mixing past and present. A cool spot for anyone snapping pics of the city's changing art scene.

La Tour Eiffel

Champ de Mars, 5 Avenue Anatole France, 75007 Paris

No visit to Paris is complete without capturing the iconic Eiffel Tower. Whether it's from Trocadéro Gardens, Champ de Mars, or the Seine Riverbanks, it always looks amazing, day and night. Don't want a basic pic standing in front of the tower? Find the best angles at Palais de Chaillot, L'Avenue de Camoëns, Port Debilly, Place Rapp, and Rue de l'Université. The quieter Rue Buenos Ayres is ideal for the golden hour: it allows you to take photos with less of a crowd, and the sun setting in the background.

Pont Alexandre III

Pont Alexandre III, 75008 Paris

This elegant bridge over the Seine is famous for its stunning architecture and sculptures. Ideal for the classic Parisian shot, especially during sunrise and sunset, it offers a romantic

↓ VILLA LÉANDRE

setting and beautiful views of the city. Plus, it's very close to the Grand Palais and Petit Palais, throwing a bit of glam into the mix.

Duperré Playground

22 Rue Duperré, 75009 Paris

Duperré Playground in Pigalle is a real treat for those seeking a burst of energy and modern street vibes. The colourful murals and a standout basketball court make it a dynamic backdrop for photo enthusiasts. The lively atmosphere, with its vivid patterns and street art, perfectly captures the modern spirit of Paris.

Pont de Bir-Hakeim

Pont de Bir-Hakeim, 75015 Paris

With its cool design and cinematic vibe, Pont de Bir-Hakeim, gives a fresh take on the Eiffel Tower. Famous for its role in *Inception*, this bridge is a dreamy spot for photographers. Stand in the middle, showcasing the bridge's structure, or take a picture of the side with the Eiffel Tower in the background. Also, the metro rides over this bridge, so if your timing is right, you'll have it in your photo for the ultimate Paris shot.

Villa Léandre

Villa Léandre, 75018 Paris

Leave the crowds and explore the charm of Villa Léandre in Montmartre. This peaceful street is lined with beautiful houses, offering a more laid-back glimpse into Parisian life. Villa Léandre provides a unique opportunity to capture the quieter, residential side of Paris. The narrow street and green surroundings make this an ideal spot for capturing the city's everyday beauty.

Rue de l'Abreuvoir

Rue de l'Abreuvoir, 75018 Paris

Wander through the enchanting streets of Montmartre and discover a photogenic street that perfectly captures the neighbourhood's timeless allure. Rue de l'Abreuvoir has a cobblestone path and the historic architecture sets the stage for captivating shots. Connected to this charming street is Place Dalida, a tranquil square named after the iconic French singer. Take a picture of the street from there, and you'll have the Sacré Cœur in the background.

The Sinking House

8 Rue Maurice Utrillo, 75018 Paris

Adding a playful twist, the Sinking House in Montmartre is an optical illusion that brings creative flair to your photo collection. Playing with different viewpoints, you create images that give the impression of a sinking building. Walk down the stairs in front of the Sacré Cœur, look to your left, tilt your phone making the grass of the hill the horizon, and it will look like the building is sinking into the ground.

Vintage photo booth in Montmartre

53 Rue des Trois Frères, 75018 Paris, fotoautomat.fr

Discover the vintage photo booth on Rue des Trois Frères in Montmartre, adding a fun element to your Parisian experience. The booth invites you to capture timeless memories. For €6, you'll get a set of four pictures with a different pose in each. The queue might be endless in summer, but there are photo booths on other locations as well.

↓ PONT ALEXANDRE III

FOOD AND DRINKS

BISTROTS & BOULANGERIES

Aux Merveilleux de Fred

Witness the pastry chefs at work, crafting their signature *merveilleux*: airy confections of meringue, cream, and chocolate shavings. You can find Aux Merveilleux de Fred on several locations in the city.

auxmerveilleux.fr

La Durée

A Parisian classic, each branch of La Durée draws crowds, especially during peak tourist season. While renowned for its *macarons*, the almond croissants are equally delightful and worth a try.

laduree.fr

Pierre Hermé

Pierre Hermé is synonymous with exquisite patisserie creations, offering a divine selection of pastries and desserts that captivate the senses. Shops can be found all over town.

pierreherme.com

Stohrer

Stohrer is the oldest bakery in Paris and invented the *baba au rhum* in 1730. It stands as a testament to centuries of pastry excellence.

51 Rue Montorgueil, 75002 Paris, stohrer.fr

Au Petit Fer à Cheval

A classic in Le Marais, Au Petit Fer à Cheval is known for its horseshoe-shaped zinc bar. Whether you're enjoying a laid-back coffee or indulging in their renowned *tarte tatin*, this spot provides a genuine taste of Paris with their non-stop kitchen from 12pm to 1am.

30 Rue Vieille du Temple, 75004 Paris

Café de Flore

A cherished gem in Saint-Germain-des-Prés, Café de Flore has been a cultural hub for artists and thinkers. This historic café is perfect for a leisurely cup of coffee or a classic French meal.

172 Boulevard Saint-Germain, 75006 Paris, cafedeflore.fr

Huguette

Huguette feels like a piece of the beach in the heart of Saint-Germain-des-Prés. Enjoy a sunny terrace with a platter of oysters and a bottle of white wine. Although primarily a seafood *bistrot*, Huguette also features some meat dishes.

81 Rue de Seine, 75006 Paris, huguette-bistro.com

↓ KB CAFÉ

↓ HARDWARE SOCIÉTÉ

Le Tournon

Le Tournon, near Jardin du Luxembourg, offers a slice of Parisian history with its traditional *bistrot* charm. It's an ideal spot to enjoy classic *bistrot* dishes and enjoy the relaxed ambiance of the city.

18 Rue Tournon, 75006 Paris, letournon.com

Le Bidou

Le Bidou stands out as a culinary treasure in Paris, inviting diners to experience authentic Parisian flavours in a warm and welcoming setting.

12 Rue Anatole de la Forge, 75017 Paris

Café des 2 Moulins

This café was made famous by the film *Le Fabuleux Destin d'Amélie Poulain*. Step into the world of Amélie as you savour a *crème brûlée* and coffee on the charming terrace of Café des 2 Moulins.

15 Rue Lepic, 75018 Paris, cafedesdeuxmoulins.fr

COFFEE & TEA

Noir

Noir is your destination for a great cup of coffee, crafted from ethically sourced Arabica beans roasted in their Parisian roastery. Stay in or grab a coffee to go. Various locations in the city.

noircoffeeshop.com

Café Kitsuné

Café Kitsuné, in the Palais-Royal Garden, provides a cosy coffee sanctuary. Sip your coffee with cake at the bar or have it to go, exploring the nearby luxury shops.

51 Galerie de Montpensier, 75001 Paris, maisonkitsune.com

Café Verlet

As the oldest coffee spot in Paris, Café Verlet has a rich history. It's a respected coffee supplier for many *bistrots*, offering a taste of the city's coffee legacy.

256 Rue Saint-Honoré, 75001 Paris, verlet.fr

Télescope

The chic and minimalist venue Télescope offers various coffee options and delightful pastries. The banana bread is a crowd-pleaser. Take a seat and unwind or grab a coffee to-go for a stroll around Palais-Royal.

5 Rue Villedo, 75001 Paris, insta @telescopecafe

Kodama

Kodama is a Japanese tea salon and shop offering an extensive selection of teas. Don't miss the chai latte, which comes highly recommended.

30 Rue Tiquetonne, 75002 Paris, kodamaparis.com

Coutume

Enjoy exotic coffee blends at Coutume Café, and choose from classic, detox veggie, or Sumatran brunch options on Saturdays and Sundays.

47 Rue de Babylone, 75007 Paris, coutumecafe.com

KB Café

For a perfect cup of coffee, head to KB Café. Their baristas expertly prepare cappuccinos and espressos and bake delightful cakes. You can buy their house blend beans to take home.

53 Avenue Trudaine, 75009 Paris, kbcoffeeroasters.com

Ten Belles

Get your caffeine fix at a hidden gem. Ten Belles serves coffee lovers using ethically sourced Arabica beans roasted in-house.

10 Rue de la Grange aux Belles, 75010 Paris, tenbelles.com

BRUNCH & LUNCH

Micho

Behind Micho's dark green façade lies an original interior and a cosy atmosphere. With seasonal vegetables or meat, a single challah (a traditional Jewish braided bread) is sufficient for lunch.

46 Rue de Richelieu, 75001 Paris, micho.fr

Season

Brunch lovers flock to Season, one of Le Marais' most beloved spots. With an extensive menu featuring both sweet and savoury options, including vegetarian and vegan choices, it's bustling, especially on Sundays.

1 Rue Charles-François Dupuis, 75003 Paris, season-paris.com

Holybelly

Have a comforting breakfast at Holybelly. From fluffy pancakes to savoury breakfast plates, it's a popular choice for a good start to the day.

5 Rue Lucien Sampaix, 75010 Paris, holybellycafe.com

Café Méricourt

Café Méricourt offers an inviting atmosphere and a menu featuring a mix of French and international cuisine. From classic croissants to hearty sandwiches, it's a delightful spot for a casual bite.

22 Rue de la Folie Méricourt, 75011 Paris, cafemericourt.com

Les Puces des Batignolles

Treat yourself at cosy neighbourhood café Les Puces de Batignolles. Their weekend brunch offers pastries, savoury delights like burgers or eggs, and your choice of coffee, tea, or a fresh juice.

110 Rue Legendre, 75017 Paris

Hardware Société

A traditional French breakfast, but with an Australian twist. Indulge in dishes like savoury mille-feuille and the fusion of French brioche with Australian lamington at Hardware Société.

10 Rue Lamarck, 75018 Paris, hardwaresociete.com

Marcel

Have a taste of New York in Paris at Marcel's 'New York style' café. It is a popular spot in charming Villa Léandre to enjoy both American and British favourites.

1 Villa Léandre, 75018 Paris, restaurantmarcel.fr

BISTRONOMIE

You'll find many revamped *bistrots* and eateries where the cuisine leans towards gastronomy while maintaining an informal *bistrot*-like atmosphere. This trend is often referred to as *bistronomie.* Curious? Some offer lunch deals on weekdays.

Nessia

Nessia offers a chef's *bistrot* experience. Although it may be on the pricey side, they offer a set lunch menu for just €15. And that includes an espresso!

6 Rue Charles-François Dupuis, 75003 Paris, restaurantnessia.com

Maison Colorova

In a light-filled space decorated in a bohemian style, Maison Colorova serves brunches and light dishes such as pastas, sandwiches, and burgers. Their lunch offer is priced from €24 to €29.

47 Rue de l'Abbé Grégoire, 75006 Paris, colorova.fr

Riviera Fuga

Floating on the Seine, Riviera Fuga offers a fancy dining experience. For a weekday lunch, you can enjoy two courses for €29 or three for €34. The cuisine is a fusion of Italian and Japanese flavours.

10 Port des Invalides, 75007 Paris, riviera-fuga.com

Coretta

Bistronomic restaurant Coretta is mentioned in the Michelin guide and serves *haute cuisine* with a blend of Mexican comfort food. The restaurant has a modern and stylish interior with picturesque views of the treetops from the second floor. The *formule déjeuner* is €32 for two courses.

151 bis Rue Cardinet, 75017 Paris, restaurantcoretta.com

STREET FOOD, SNACKS & SANDWICHES

Bältis

At Bältis, you'll find delicious Lebanese-inspired ice cream flavours, including pistachio, sesame, and unique options like *thyme and olive oil*. They serve from two shops in the city.

baltisparis.com

Bollynan

Indulge in Indian street food at Bollynan, where the house specialty is the *butter chicken 'nanwich'* (fusion of naan and a sandwich). Craving something sweet? The *nan* with Nutella and coconut shavings is delightful. Two locations in Paris.

bollynan.com

Chipotle

Chipotle serves deliciously fresh food. Indulge in a custom-made burrito, tacos, or a Mexican bowl for a flavoursome food experience. There are three branches in Paris.

chipotle.fr

Kurry Up

Serving Indian street food, Kurry Up offers traditional Indian dishes like *chicken masala* alongside the option to customise your meal. On various locations in the city.

kurryup.fr

PNY

PNY serves gourmet burgers with flair. They offer a diverse range, including vegetarian and fish options, all with quality ingredients. You'll find PNY on various locations in the city.

pnyburger.com

PITOT ARTISANALES
FAITES SUR PLACE
פיתות ביתיות
פרגית

Schwartz's Deli

Modern and trendy. Schwartz's Deli delivers with their delicious burgers and sandwiches. Their pastrami sandwiches and cheesecake are especially delicious. You'll find them on a few locations.

schwartzsdeli.fr

Breizh Café

Known for having the best *crêpes* in Paris, Breizh Café is a must-visit for *crêpe* enthusiasts. The bustling restaurant in le Marais offers an extensive selection, both savoury and sweet.

109 Rue Vieille du Temple, 75003 Paris, breizhcafe.com

Berthillon

Berthillon serves Paris' best ice cream, with its original shop located on Île Saint Louis. With an extensive selection of flavours, it's a must-try.

29-31 Rue Saint-Louis en l'Île, 75004 Paris, berthillon.fr

Pat's US Hot Dogs

Craving a quick bite? This tiny outlet serves unexpectedly delicious hotdogs. At Pat's, you'll pick your hotdog type and combine the toppings you like for a tasty snack.

56 Rue du Roi de Sicile, 75004 Paris

Rue des Rosiers

Venture to Rue des Rosiers for Middle Eastern cuisine. L'As du Fallafel has often been crowned as the top falafel spot and its popularity will require you to queue. If you are in more of a hurry, there are plenty of other good eateries on this road.

Rue des Rosiers, 75004 Paris

Au P'tit Grec

Located in the charming Rue Mouffetard, Au P'tit Grec stands out as the go-to *crêperie* in the area. The street is filled with *crêperies*, but this one has earned its reputation for serving delicious *crêpes* in a warm and inviting setting.

68 Rue Mouffetard, 75005 Paris, auptitgrec.com

Mersea

Renowned chef Olivier Bellin introduces a street food seafood restaurant concept with fresh and sustainable catches. The standout item at Mersea is the delicate fish & chips.

53-57 Rue de Grenelle, 75007 Paris, merseaparis.com

Baldoria

Italian cuisine in a street food style – a great option if you're craving authentic Italian flavours but are on a budget. Baldoria's pizza slices are priced from €2.80 to €4.00.

51 Rue Notre Dame de Lorette, 75009 Paris, baldoria.marketplace.dood.com

Galbar

Galbar offers a unique twist to *crêpes*, serving them in unconventional ways. From sweet options inspired by French desserts, like the *crêpe crème brûlée*, to creatively crafted savoury choices, each has its own special touch.

50 Rue du Faubourg Poissonnière, 75010 Paris, galbar.fr

Nomas Tacos

Nomas Tacos offers affordable and tasty Mexican fare, perfect for a quick bite. While its terrace is small, it's an ideal spot for take-away tacos, quesadillas, and burritos.

44 Rue du Faubourg Saint-Denis, 75010 Paris, nomas-tacos.com

Krügen Gardette

Enjoy the cosy atmosphere of Krügen Gardette, with a charming mix of Breton and French vibes. Their menu features a delightful array of *galettes* and *crêpes*.

4 Rue du Général Renault, 75011 Paris, krugenparis.com

CHEZ JANOU

Bulot Bulot

Go to oyster bar Bulot Bulot for oysters or other seafood, such as crab. It provides good value for money, especially if you visit on Wednesday evenings when oysters are priced at €1 each.

83 Rue des Martyrs, 75018 Paris, bulotbulot.fr

Ruisseau

Claiming to serve the best burgers in town, Ruisseau offers a wide selection of burgers, including vegetarian and fish options. With its proud declaration and satisfied customers, it's a must-visit.

65 Rue du Ruisseau, 75018 Paris, leruisseauburger.com

DINNER TIME

Les Amis des Messina

Les Amis de Messina brings the taste of Italy to Paris on two locations, with its selection of quality products and fresh pasta dishes. In an inviting atmosphere, you'll enjoy small bites or pasta dishes.

lesamisdesmessina.com

Big Mamma Group

Big Mamma Group is a collection of Italian restaurants known for their stunning decor and mouth-watering dishes. Pink Mamma, for instance, features four floors and a speakeasy in the basement, serving delicious Napolitan pizzas and truffle-infused pasta dishes.

bigmammagroup.com

Côté Sushi

A blend of Japanese and Peruvian cuisine? You'll find it at Côté Sushi. They combine the precision of Japanese cooking with the exotic and spicy flavours of Peru. On various locations in Paris.

cotesushi.com

Ippudo

With multiple locations, Ippudo is renowned for its ramen, particularly the pork-based *tonkotsu ramen*.

ippudo.fr

Melt

Catering to meat enthusiasts, Melt brings Texan barbecue to Paris. They adopt the culinary values of Texas by smoking all their meats over oak wood at low temperatures for long hours. They currently have three restaurants in Paris.

meltslowsmokedbarbecue.com

Poké Bar

Delicious poke bowls, with options from the menu, and the flexibility to customise your own bowl according to your preferences. Poké Bar is found on multiple locations in the city.

pokebar.fr

Popine

Popine offers amazing pizzas at slightly higher prices. But if you're looking for top-notch pizza with exceptional flavours, Popine is the place to go – you can find them in two places in the city.

insta @popineparis

Trantranzai

Sichuan cuisine, featuring dishes like the *dan dan noodle soup*. Trantranzai has a charming interior that complements the authentic flavours. On two Paris locations.

trantranzai.fr

Bistrot Victoires

Hidden behind Palais-Royal, Bistrot Victoires offers an affordable dining experience with classics like *canard confit* and *escargots*. The vintage interior and outdoor terrace provide a welcoming setting.

6 Rue de la Vrillière, 75001 Paris

Kodawari

Kodawari Tsukiji is a ramen restaurant with a décor reminiscent of a Tokyo fish market. Their ramen, prepared in fish broth, is a must-try, especially the chef's special.

12 Rue de Richelieu, 75001 Paris, kodawari-ramen.com

Rue Sainte-Anne

The 1st arrondissement's Japanese quarter, centred around Rue Sainte-Anne, is brimming with Japanese restaurants. We recommend Juji-ya for a delicious bento box.

Rue Sainte-Anne, 75001 Paris

Udon Bistro Kunitoraya

Known for its Udon noodles, Udon Bistro Kunitoraya is where Chef Kunitoraya served the first Udon noodles in France. Get a taste of authentic Japanese cuisine.

1 Rue Villédo, 75001 Paris, kunitoraya.com

Comme un Bouillon

True to its name, Comme un Bouillon provides a warm and comforting dining experience, embracing the essence of French culinary tradition with a diverse menu catering to various tastes.

17 Rue de Choiseul, 75002 Paris, commeunbouillon.com

Chez Janou

For a taste of Provencal delights, dine at Chez Janou. Try *brandade de morue* and lavender-infused *crème brûlée*. The charming *bistrot* captures the essence of Southern French cuisine and atmosphere, with intimate interiors and and inviting terrace.

2 Rue Roger Verlomme, 75003 Paris, chezjanou.com

Pain Vin Fromages

Indulge in a winter feast with comforting mountain dishes like *raclette*, *fondue*, or *tartiflette*. Pain Vin Fromages is a perfect spot if you're craving hearty and satisfying flavours.

3 Rue Geoffroy l'Angevin, 75004 Paris, painvinfromages.com

Pastasuta

For the essence of Italian cuisine, offering authentic fresh pasta dishes, go to Pastasuta. With different options for your preferred pasta type, you're guaranteed a satisfying meal.

2 Rue de la Coutellerie, 75004 Paris, pastasuta.fr

Foyer Vietnam

Find authentic Vietnamese cuisine at Foyer Vietnam. With an array of main courses and appetisers, it transports you to Asia for just a moment.

80 Rue Monge, 75005 Paris, foyer-vietnam.org

La Maison du Dim Sum

Are you a dim sum enthusiast? La Maison du Dim Sum offers tasty dishes. Choose the discovery menu option, a delightful mix of dumplings and traditional delights.

4 Rue des Fossés Saint-Jacques, 75005 Paris, lamaisondudimsum.com

CHARTIER

Oi Sushi

A la carte sushi is the highlight at Oi Sushi, especially during lunch hours, offering reasonably priced options.

7 Rue Mouffetard, 75005 Paris, oisushi-mouffetard.fr

Chez Germaine

Chez Germaine welcomes diners with the charm of traditional French hospitality. Enjoy classic French tastes in a cosy atmosphere, where the menu reflects a personal touch and a commitment to culinary excellence.

30 Rue Pierre Leroux, 75007 Paris, chezgermaineparis.fr

Mandoobar

Mandoobar is the go-to spot for *mandoos*, Korean dumplings. It's listed in the Michelin guide and surprisingly affordable.

7 Rue d'Édimbourg, 75008 Paris, mandoobar.fr

Miss Kô

Miss Kô offers an intriguing dining experience with its fusion of Asian flavours and modern atmosphere.

49-51 Avenue George V, 75008 Paris, miss-ko.com

Bouillon Chartier

A true Parisian institution, Bouillon Chartier has been serving classic dishes in a vintage setting since 1896. It's a timeless *bistrot* where history meets hearty French dining. You'll find Bouillons in Pigalle and République as well.

7 Rue du Faubourg Montmartre, 75009 Paris, bouillon-chartier.com

Saam

A small Korean restaurant with an open kitchen, known for its *boa*. Diners at Saam can choose from various menus, promising a delightful experience.

59 bis Rue de Lancry, 75010 Paris, insta @saamparis

Yummy

Located near Gare du Nord and Gare de l'Est, Yummy is perfect for a pre-train meal or take-away. The diverse menu features Asian cuisine from sushi to ramen and bubble tea.

8 Rue du 8 Mai 1945, 75010 Paris, yummy.fr

La Cantine Coréenne

Offering an extensive menu at affordable prices, La Cantine Coréenne is a haven for Korean food lovers, especially for its lunch menu options.

58 Avenue de la République, 75011 Paris, republique.lacantinecoreenne.fr

Chez Ravioli Chen Chen

Offering *baos* for €1.25 and shareable dumplings for €6, Chez Ravioli Chen Chen is a cosy eatery. It's run by a Chinese couple who poured their hearts into creating a budget-friendly dining experience.

54 Avenue Philippe Auguste, 75011 Paris

Little Hanoi

Little Hanoi offers authentic Vietnamese cuisine, featuring mains around €12.50 and appetisers around €5. Despite its small size, the restaurant is a popular choice, often with a queue outside.

9 Rue de Mont-Louis, 75011 Paris, parishanoi.fr

Yaaï Thaï

Yaaï Thaï boasts an extensive Thai menu, a delightful interior, and reasonable prices, making it a top choice.

22 Rue Daguerre, 75014 Paris, yaai-thai.com

Noura Marceau

Noura Marceau offers a *bistrot*-style Lebanese dining experience, with an array of mezze options perfect for sharing among friends and family.

27 Avenue Marceau, 75016 Paris, noura.com

Le Petit Cambodge

For a fusion of French and Cambodian flavours, visit Le Petit Cambodge. The diverse menu features *bao buns*, curries, and spring rolls.

25 Rue Guy Môquet, 75017 Paris, lepetitcambodge.fr

Bouillon Pigalle

Bouillon Pigalle offers traditional French cuisine with a modern twist. In the vibrant Pigalle district, it presents a perfect fusion of flavours in a stylish setting.

22 Bd de Clichy, 75018 Paris, bouillonlesite.com/bouillon-pigalle

Le Refuge des Fondues

Le Refuge des Fondues offers a unique dining experience with communal tables and playful *fondue* servings. This Montmartre restaurant provides a memorable and interactive culinary adventure.

17 Rue des Trois Frères, 75018 Paris, insta @refugedesfondus_montmartre

Le Consulat

Historic Montmartre café Le Consulat preserves the artistic spirit of bygone days. Enjoy traditional French dishes, including *gratinéed* onion soup, in a charming and nostalgic setting.

18 Rue Norvins, 75018 Paris, insta @restaurantleconsulat

L'Artisan Libanais

L'Artisan Libanais presents a vegetarian tasting menu, showcasing the richness and diversity of Lebanese cuisine.

91 Rue de Belleville, 75019 Paris, artisan-libanais.com

Le Bastringue

Le Bastringue invites diners to enjoy a reasonably priced midday formula, offering a choice of two or three courses. In a charming *bistrot* setting, it provides a satisfying culinary escape.

67 Quai de la Seine, 75019 Paris, lebastringue.business.site

Dame Jane

Dame Jane in Belleville offers a dining experience with an ever-changing menu and rotating chefs. The intimate restaurant showcases culinary talents before they launch into their own ventures.

39 Rue Ramponeau, 75020 Paris, insta @damejaneresidence

BRING THE PARENTS

Langosteria

A luxurious seafood restaurant known for its extensive wine cellar. Langosteria is situated on the rooftop of the prestigious Le Cheval Blanc hotel and offers breathtaking views of the Seine.

8 Quai du Louvre, 75001 Paris, langosteria.com

Frenchie

Earning a Michelin star in 2019, Frenchie is a renowned establishment in Paris. It is run by Gregory Marchand, nick-named 'Frenchie' during his time in Jamie Oliver's kitchens, and offers French-inspired dishes with an international flair.

5 Rue du Nil, 75002 Paris, frenchie-ruedunil.com

Gigi

Delightful Milanese cuisine in a beautiful rooftop restaurant. Gigi's stunning interior is complemented by an even better ambiance on the terrace, with views of the Eiffel Tower.

15 Avenue Montaigne, 75008 Paris, gigi-restaurant.com

LOCATION
GESTION

MARCEL

GOING OUT

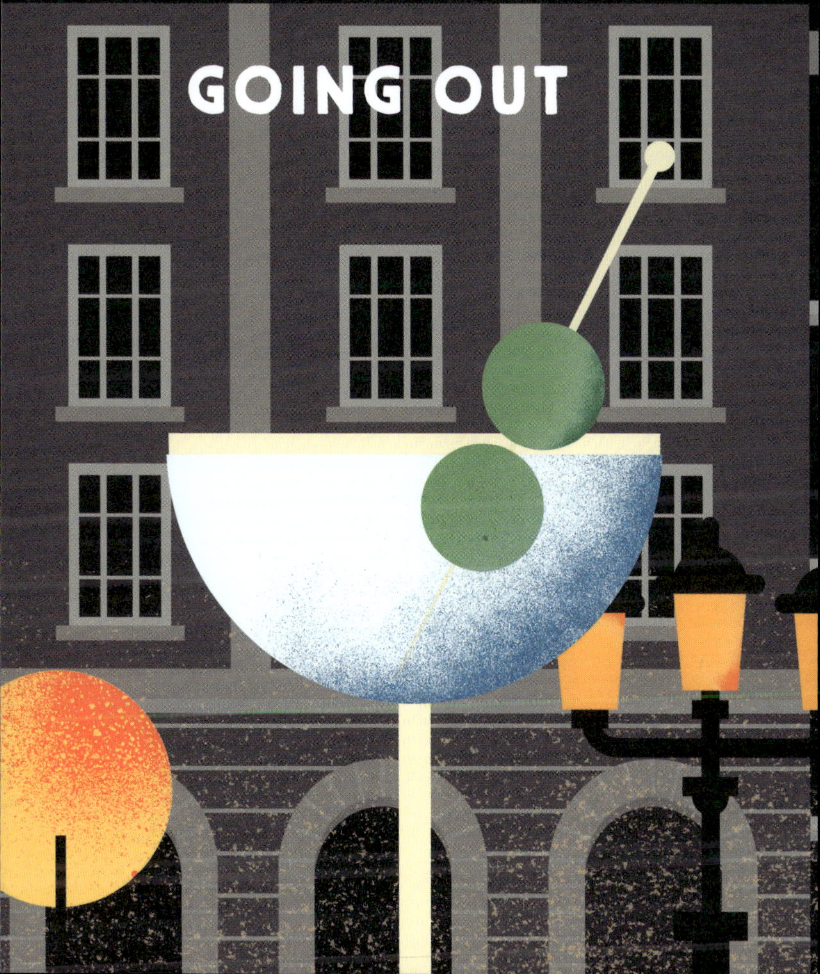

APÉRO

During the summer months, Paris comes alive with vibrant pop-up terraces with a festival-like atmosphere. Decorated with wooden pallet chairs and cheerful accents, accompanied by DJs playing tunes, and a variety of street food offerings, these terraces attract locals and visitors alike. Explore what's on offer by searching for *terrasses estivales ephemeres Paris*, with websites like Sortir à Paris and Paris Je t'aime providing lists of events and locations.

Le 17.45

Opening its doors daily at a quarter to six, each location of Le 17.45 invites you to craft your own charcuterie and cheese boards. Choose from a variety of meats, cheeses, and even a veggie option.

le17-45.fr

Berliner Wunderbar

Berliner Wunderbar (on three locations in the city) invites you to savour delicious German beer, accompanied by a pretzel or *wurst sandwich*. Weekends often feature DJs, adding to the lively atmosphere.

berlinerwunderbar.com

Le Perchoir

Discover multiple beautiful rooftop bars under the name of Le Perchoir. Treat yourself to a cocktail and admire the cityscape while appreciating their commitment to sustainability.

leperchoir.fr

Brique Machine

Step into the world of Brique Machine, a brewery where everything is painted pink. Beyond its charming décor, they offer a variety of specialty beers brewed in-house.

161 Rue Montmartre, 75002 Paris, briquehouse.com

La Cordonnerie

Offering the most budget-friendly drinks in Paris, La Cordonnerie attracts a diverse crowd, including students and creatives, to its cosy tavern ambiance.

142 Rue Saint-Denis, 75002 Paris

Place de la Contrescarpe

A charming square frequented by students, Place de la Contrescarpe offers various bars with enticing happy hour deals. Go over to the cosy pub Le Requin Chagrin or Café Delmas for a drink.

Place de la Contrescarpe, 75005 Paris

Le Bar 21

Offering affordability without compromising on taste, Le Bar 21 presents boards starting at €10. Along with affordable cocktails and beers, it's a budget-friendly choice for a casual evening out.

21 Rue Bergère, 75009 Paris

Café A

Housed in a former monastery, Café A provides a serene garden setting ideal for an *apéro*, especially during the summer months.

148 Rue du Faubourg Saint-Martin, 75010 Paris, cafea.fr

↓ CAFÉ A

↓ MONCOEUR BELLEVILLE

↓ LES CAVES POPULAIRES

O Lieu de

Ideal for an *apéro*, O Lieu de offers wonderful cheese and charcuterie boards or tapas to accompany your drinks. They offer a good selection of quality wines and tasty beers.

6 Rue Jean-Pierre Timbaud, 75011 Paris, olieude.net

Oplato

The focus at Oplato is on indulgent platters, featuring meat, cheese, and vegan options. You can even customise your own board. Choose a cocktail or glass of wine to go with it.

69 Rue de Charonne, 75011 Paris, oplato.com

Ground Control

Located in the historic train depot of Gare de Lyon, at Ground Control you'll find food trucks, bars, shops, and exhibitions that fill the space creatively. Some vendors even set up shop inside old buses.

81 Rue du Charolais, 75012 Paris, groundcontrolparis.com

Le Hasard Ludique

Located in an old tram station, Le Hasard Ludique serves as a feminist cultural hub. In summer, its expansive terrace along the tram tracks is perfect for an *apéro*.

128 Avenue de Saint-Ouen, 75018 Paris, lehasardludique.paris

La Bellevilloise

Featuring a spacious hall filled with olive trees, La Bellevilloise is perfect for an *apéro* or an evening of dancing to hip-hop, soul, and funk. Look out for their occasional Classics Only night.

19-21 Rue Boyer, 75020 Paris, labellevilloise.com

Moncœur Belleville

For a breathtaking view over Paris rooftops, go to Moncœur Belleville and enjoy spectacular sunsets from the terrace. Or visit their exhibitions, lectures, and musical evenings indoors.

1 Rue des Envierges, 75020 Paris, moncoeurbelleville.com

Bouillon Belge

Quench your thirst with a selection of around thirty Belgian beers on tap at Bouillon Belge. With additional options in the fridge, this is a beer lover's paradise.

6 Rue Planchat, 75020 Paris

WINE & COCKTAILS

Indiana Café

Indiana Café is a cocktail bar with several locations across Paris. During happy hour, you can enjoy delicious cocktails on the terrace at a great price. Don't miss out on their tasty nachos!

indianacafe.fr

Bisou.

At Bisou. you won't find a menu. Tell the bartender what you're in the mood for, and they'll craft you a custom cocktail. Everything around you is beautifully pink.

15 Boulevard du Temple, 75003 Paris, bar-bisou.com

Candelaria

While a bit pricey, Candelaria offers exceptional cocktails. This speakeasy is hidden behind the door of a small taco joint with a green façade.

52 Rue de Saintonge, 75003 Paris, candelaria-paris.com

Le Mary Celeste

A popular spot in Le Marais, Le Mary Celeste is a trendy cocktail and oyster bar where you can also enjoy a beer or glass of wine.

1 Rue Commines, 75003 Paris, lemaryceleste.com

↓ TIGER

↓ TIGER

↓ CAFÉ A

Little Red Door

Little Red Door is an original speakeasy where you enter through, you guessed it, a small red door into a cosy, dimly lit space. The bar has a chic, modern ambiance.

60 Rue Charlot, 75003 Paris, lrdparis.com

Tiger

Tiger stands out with its mosaic floors, jungle-themed wallpaper, and multi-level layout. It's a gin lover's paradise, offering a wide selection of G&Ts.

13 Rue Princesse, 75006 Paris, tiger-paris.com

Abricot

Described as a 'fun, creative cocktails & plant-based bites' spot, Abricot offers tasty cocktails. They pride themselves on being a California-Brooklyn-style bar, run by women and catering to everyone.

189 Rue Saint-Maur, 75010 Paris, abricotbar.com

La Curieuse Compagnie

A delightful wine bar. The ambiance is relaxed, with an interior decorated with wine bottles, adding to its charm.

32 Rue de l'Échiquier, 75010 Paris

Les Petits Crus

Les Petits Crus gives an experience reminiscent of your school days, but with wine. Wines are served in test tubes, and cheeses on a chalkboard, creating an interactive tasting session. Additionally, they offer an escape game experience.

13 Rue Saint Sabin, 75011 Paris, lespetitscrus.com

Le Baron Rouge

Known as possibly the cheapest wine bar in Paris, Le Baron Rouge is a favourite spot for locals, especially at weekends and during oyster season.

1 Rue Théophile Roussel, 75012 Paris, lebaronrouge.net

Les Caves Populaires

An inviting spot to enjoy a cheese platter and a glass of wine. Les Caves Populaires is a cosy neighbourhood café, popular with students.

22 Rue des Dames, 75017 Paris, insta @lescavespopulaires

Combat

Run by women, cocktail bar Combat not only serves delicious cocktails but also embodies the strength of feminism. The name pays homage to the Belleville district and the feminist struggle, *le combat féministe*.

63 Rue de Belleville, 75019 Paris, insta @combat.belleville

QUEER

The Marais neighbourhood hosts several gay bars. Rue des Archives is home to larger bars like Cox, which is ideal for a night out. Le Ju, perfect for *apéro*, is known for its rainbow umbrellas. And on Rue de Verrerie you'll find Les Souffleurs, a reputable gay bar. Explore more LGBTQI+ friendly bars, clubs, and events on

parislgbt.com.

Club Banana Café

For themed nights near Chatelet, go to Club Banana Café. It attracts a diverse crowd of locals and tourists. Suitable for both *apéro* and a night out.

13 Rue de la Ferronnerie, 75001 Paris

La Mutinerie

A feminist bar and space exclusively managed by and for the LGBTQI+ community.

La Mutinerie is close to Centre Pompidou and is always bustling. Nearby, you'll find a similar venue called Le Bar'Ouf.

176-178 Rue Saint-Martin, 75003 Paris, lamutinerie.eu

Sister Midnight

Award-winning inclusive cocktail bar Sister Midnight in Pigalle, is reviving the area's glam rock roots. It offers chic decor and regular drag and burlesque performances.

4 Rue Viollet-le-Duc, 75009 Paris, sistermidnightparis.com

Madame Arthur

Madame Arthur opened in 1945 as the first drag cabaret in Paris. It features a new show every week.

75 bis Rue des Martyrs, 75018 Paris, madamearthur.fr

CLUBS

Café Oz

Café Oz is a chain of dance cafés with multiple locations across Paris. With its Australian-inspired décor and lively vibe, Café Oz offers a relaxed setting for dancing.

cafe-oz.com

Rex Club

Located in the basement of the iconic Le Grand Rex cinema, is Rex Club. A legendary venue that has hosted some of the world's top DJs and electronic music events.

5 Boulevard Poissonnière, 75002 Paris, rexclub.com

Le Carmen

Historical charm is blended with nightlife vibes at Le Carmen. Housed in a former brothel, its interior features columns and statues, creating a unique backdrop for hip-hop nights.

34 Rue Duperré, 75009 Paris, le-carmen.fr

Badaboum

A hotspot for house and techno in Paris. With its sleek design and state-of-the-art sound system, Badaboum is a haven for electronic music lovers.

2bis Rue des Taillandiers, 75011 Paris, badaboum.paris

Supersonic

Supersonic stands out for its diverse music offerings. With free entry on weekdays and affordable weekend cover charges, it's a budget-friendly option for clubbers in Paris.

9 Rue Biscornet, 75012 Paris, supersonic-club.fr

Petit Bain

A unique club experience on a floating barge on the Seine. Petit Bain hosts a variety of concerts, DJ sets, and cultural events.

7 Port de la Gare, 75013 Paris, petitbain.org

La Station – Gare des mines

La Station – Gare des Mines is a dynamic cultural space housed in an old railway station. It's renowned for its underground electronic music scene and experimental events.

29 Avenue de la Porte d'Aubervilliers, 75018 Paris, lastation.paris

La Machine du Moulin Rouge

Situated in the iconic Moulin Rouge district, La Machine du Moulin Rouge is a popular club known for its diverse line-up of events and performances.

90 Boulevard de Clichy, 75018 Paris, lamachinedumoulinrouge.com

à la folie

Located in Parc de la Villette, à la folie transforms into a vibrant club venue in weekends, but it also hosts unique events like Bingo Drag Apéro on Sundays.

26 Avenue Corentin Cariou, 75019 Paris, alafolie.paris

SHOPPING

HOW TO DRESS LIKE A LOCAL

Parisian style isn't about chasing trends; it's all about timeless elegance. The Parisienne knows what looks good on her and she creates a style for herself. It is, after all, more interesting to be yourself than to just follow a trend. Discover your own style and signature items and wear them with confidence: you will be fine.

Now, if you want to blend in like a true Parisian, keep it simple and effortlessly chic. Think neutral colours and oversized fits. Every Parisienne has a killer pair of jeans – the Parisienne will only wear skirts and dresses during heatwaves – and you can't go wrong with a crisp white shirt. Throw on a leather jacket for some edge or opt for a classy smoking jacket for a touch of sophistication.

In the quest for authenticity, some Parisiennes cut their own hair, aiming for that perpetually quasi-messy look. And you won't catch them flaunting brand logos – simplicity and individuality are key. Leave the berets, shorts, minis, and crop tops at home.

You can't nail the Parisian look without a stylish long coat and oversized sunglasses for a dash of mystery. Add your personal touch with a silk scarf, some jewellery, or a chic bag slung over your shoulder – that is where you'll shine.

Now, for the guys, Parisian style is all about keeping it low-key yet classy. Forget flashy logos and bright colours – the Parisian man prefers a subtle, personal vibe. Navy is his jam, and he's all about refinement without going over the top. Mixing high-end with affordable pieces is the Parisian way. Rocking a tailored suit jacket with a pair of jeans or a modest watch is the ultimate in casual sophistication.

True Parisian cool is all about looking effortlessly stylish, you don't want anyone to think you're trying too hard. It's not just about the clothes; it's about the attitude – that relaxed, refined vibe that is quintessentially Parisian.

VINTAGE, FLEA MARKETS & SECOND-HAND

Puces de Saint-Ouen

138-140 Rue des Rosiers, 93400 Saint-Ouen, marcheauxpuces-saintouen.com

Located in the north of the city, the world's largest flea market awaits. Spanning fifteen markets and halls, you'll discover over two thousand shops, each with its own unique character and distinctive atmosphere. Collectors and vintage enthusiasts will find joy, as each shop is more beautiful than the last. Shopkeepers are aware of the value of their merchandise, but bargaining is always an option.

Puces de Vanves

Avenue Georges-Lafenestre / Avenue Marc-Sangnier, 75014 Paris, pucesdevanves.com

Located in the south of Paris, Puces de Vanves is a charming flea market set in a more intimate environment. With a diverse array of vintage finds, from clothing to furniture, it's a delightful spot for treasure hunters. You can visit the flea market in weekends, from morning until lunchtime.

Puces de Montreuil

Avenue du Professeur André Lemierre, 75020 Paris, lespuces-portedemontreuil.com pucesdevanves.com

Situated on the outskirts of the city, Puces de Montreuil is one of the largest flea markets in Paris. Boasting a diverse mix of items, it's an ideal destination for those seeking unique vintage pieces and quirky collectibles.

NTAGE BOUTIQUE

Puces d'Aligre

Place d'Aligre, 75012 Paris, pucesaligre.unblog.fr

This flea market in the lively Aligre neighbourhood offers a vibrant mix of antiques, vintage clothing, and eclectic knick-knacks. For locals as well as visitors, Puces d'Aligre is a great place to explore.

Village Popincourt

villagepopincourt.paris

In this neighbourhood you'll find several vintage shops, including Ol'digger, known as the funky *friperie* (second-hand shop). Shift Depot and Urban Exchange also stand out, offering modern styles and a sustainable approach to fashion.

BIS Boutique Solidaire

bisboutiquesolidaire.fr

Tucked away in the heart of Paris, BIS Boutique Solidaire is perfect for those seeking curated fashion gems. From retro clothes to timeless accessories, the shop offers a carefully selected collection at an affordable price. The ambiance is modern, making it a delightful spot to browse and discover hidden treasures. Four shops in Paris.

Bobby

insta @bobby.in.paris

Bobby offers vintage items of both reputable and lesser-known brands. The items can get pricey, so they are only attainable if you have some money left to spend. With brands from Gucci to Miu Miu and everything needed to build a timeless outfit, there's something for everyone at either one of Bobby's two locations.

Emmaüs Défi

emmaus-defi.org

Emmaüs Défi, a chain of vintage stores in Paris, goes beyond retail. Their goal is to serve as a job reintegration and remobilisation project, helping vulnerable people to find their place in society.

FREE'P'STAR

insta @freepstar_officiel

With multiple locations across the city, FREE'P'STAR is a chain of shops offering affordable vintage clothes and accessories. It's a budget-friendly option for those who love the thrill of the hunt.

Guerrisol

guerrisol.fr

With forty years of history and sixteen locations in Paris, Guerrisol is a vintage giant. Whether you're looking for H&M, Adidas, or luxury brands such as Ralph Lauren, Guerrisol has a vast selection of clothes, accessories, and more.

Kilo Shop

kilo-shop.com

Kilo Shop reinvented second-hand shopping by pricing items by weight. From clothes to accessories, visitors can curate their style, and pay based on the weight of the treasures they found. It's a playful and budget-friendly approach to vintage shopping, attracting a diverse crowd seeking both affordability and individuality.

Le Relais, La Boutique

lerelaislaboutique.com

Le Relais, La Boutique, formerly Ding Fring, is a chain of shops known for their commitment to sustainability. Offering a mix of second-hand and vintage items, it's a great choice for eco-conscious shoppers seeking stylish finds.

ZXSBN6DD3VZBGSY

insta @zxsbn6dd3vzbgsy

Playfully named after a Wi-Fi code, those shops are the most affordable *friperies* in Paris, offering clothes at incredibly low prices. You'll find not only budget-friendly pieces but also well-known brands such as Dolce & Gabbana and Yves Saint Laurent.

Episode

12-16 Rue Tiquetonne, 75002 Paris, episode.eu

Known for its diverse and affordable second-hand finds, Episode is a hotspot for fashion-forward individuals with a penchant for unique pieces. The shop carries a diverse range of clothes and accessories from various eras, allowing shoppers to craft distinctive looks that tell their own style stories.

Kiliwatch

64 Rue Tiquetonne, 75002 Paris, insta @kiliwatch.paris

Known for its trendy vintage and second-hand clothes, Kiliwatch is a chic *boutique* near Les Halles. The shop seamlessly blends contemporary fashion with timeless vintage pieces, creating a unique shopping experience.

Retro

20 Rue de Turbigo, 75002 Paris, insta @retro_paris2

With 125m^2 of vintage treasures, Retro offers a vast range of items, including a dedicated section for children's clothing.

Nice Piece

76 Rue Charlot, 75003 Paris

True to its name, Nice Piece is a vintage store that prides itself on offering an excellent selection of high-quality and unique pieces. From clothes to accessories, it's a dream for vintage enthusiasts looking for something special.

Seven Boys and Girls

7 Rue du Pont aux Choux, 75003 Paris, insta @ sevenboysandgirls

For fashion enthusiasts, Seven Boys and Girls in the Marais district is known for its curated collection of clothes and accessories from various eras, providing an amazing shopping experience.

The Vintage

25 Boulevard du Temple, 75003 Paris, insta @the_vintage_mtc

Specialising in Vintage Levi's, this store is a denim lover's paradise. Discover a curated collection of timeless denim pieces and other vintage fashion items.

Aux comptoirs du chineur

49 Rue Saint-Paul, 75004 Paris

A haven for random finds, this shop offers a diverse mix of items, from records and shoes to quirky pins. At Aux comptoirs du chineur you will stumble upon interesting treasures.

Hippy Market

41 Rue du Temple, 75004 Paris, hippy-market.fr

Located in Le Marais, Hippy Market is a vintage shop specialising in 70s clothes with a splash of 80s and 90s. Offering colourful and standout pieces, it captures the spirit of the Flower Power era.

The King Of Frip

33 Rue du Roi de Sicile, 75004 Paris

A dream for vintage lovers, The King Of Frip offers carefully selected second-hand clothes. The shop is known for its diverse collection, ranging from stylish apparel to furniture finds.

Rue de la Verrerie

Rue de la Verrerie, 75004 Paris

Rue de la Verrerie, in the heart of Paris, is an oasis for vintage enthusiasts. This charming street has a collection of unique vintage shops, each offering a distinct shopping experience.

Compil

84 Rue Mouffetard, 75005 Paris, compilstore.fr

A blend of vintage and upcycling, Compil is both a shop and an atelier where items are creatively enhanced.

Thanx God I'm a V.I.P.

12 Rue de Lancry, 75010 Paris, thanxgod.com

Situated in the trendy Marais district, this vintage shop is a favourite among fashion-forward individuals. Offering carefully selected pieces, it's a go-to spot for those looking to make a stylish statement with fashion.

Belle Lurette

5 Rue du Marché Popincourt, 75011 Paris

For a touch of French vintage elegance, Belle Lurette is a must-visit boutique. With a refined selection, this shop exudes sophistication and charm. Each item tells a tale of timeless fashion, making it a favourite for those who appreciate the art of vintage dressing.

La Frange à l'envers

81 Rue Saint-Maur, 75011 Paris, lafrangealenvers.fr

A vintage shop in Passage Saint-Maur, offering a mix of high-end Parisian brands like Maje, haute couture items, and even pieces from mainstream brands like Zara. La Frange à l'envers is known for its organisation by colour as well as its stylish interior.

Lapin Boutique

9 Rue Oberkampf, 75011 Paris, lapin-boutique.com

As an independent and responsible vintage and designer clothes shop, Lapin Vintage focuses on the 60s and 70s aesthetic. While prices may be higher, the niche and carefully chosen collection make it a one-of-a-kind shopping destination.

Urban Vintage

50 Rue du Faubourg du Temple, 75011 Paris, urbanvintageparis.com

Go to Urban Vintage if you are looking for urban and trendy vintage pieces. For fashion-forward individuals looking to add a touch of retro flair to their wardrobe.

By Flowers

86 Rue des Martyrs, 75018 Paris, insta @byflowersparis

Tucked away in the 18th *arrondissement*, By Flowers is a vintage boutique stocking carefully selected clothes and accessories. The shop exudes a bohemian and retro vibe, attracting fashion lovers seeking one-of-a-kind pieces.

Chine Machine

100 Rue des Martyrs, 75018 Paris, chinemachinevintage.com

A gem in the vintage scene, Chine Machine is a treasure trove of second-hand items, including clothes, accessories, and home decor. It's a popular spot for those who appreciate a mix of styles from different decades.

STREETWEAR

Blvck

emea.blvck.com

A lifestyle and accessories brand founded by a French designer, known for its all-black clothing for men and women. Blvck focuses on quality and design, daring you to live life on your own terms, free from vanity.

Human With Attitude

humanwithattitude.com

If you are looking for quality clothing that allows you to stand out, check out Human With Attitude. The brand's passion is to create powerful pieces that combine comfort and style, designed to celebrate individualism and diversity.

Ombre Parisienne

ombre-parisienne.com

Capturing the street culture of Paris, Ombre Parisienne draws inspiration from music, sports, fashion, art, and film. As a sustainable brand, it prioritises the use of organic cottons, with fabrics produced and garments tailored in France.

Project x Paris

projectxparis.com

At Project x Paris, streetwear is a way of life. Launched by two French designers, the streetwear brand offers a broad collection of clothes and accessories for men and women. From casual and comfortable basics to unique and stylish streetwear, PXP combines minimalism with street culture.

Sixth June

sixthjune.com

With a genuine connection to the community, Sixth June plays a pioneering role in foreseeing, embracing, and embodying the Paris streetwear culture. The brand successfully united some of the city's most influential creatives.

North Hill

30 Rue du Vertbois, 75003 Paris, northhill.fr

A creative and sustainable brand showcasing the new couture of North Paris. The young team designs high-quality menswear with an honest and independent approach, working closely with local Parisian workshops.

DEPARTMENT STORES

Samaritaine

9 Rue de la Monnaie, 75001 Paris, dfs.com

Located near the Seine, this *grand magasin* seamlessly blends Art Nouveau and Art Deco styles. Following extensive restoration, luxury brands such as Dior and Gucci are now housed at Samaritaine. You must go inside, even if it's just to take a quick look.

BHV Marais

52 Rue de Rivoli, 75004 Paris, bhv.fr

BHV, short for Bazar de l'Hôtel de Ville, is a beloved Parisian institution in the charming Marais district. Across its seven different floors in various buildings, you'll find everything you want and need. Go all the way up to the rooftop bar, Le Perchoir Marais.

Le Bon Marché Rive Gauche

24 Rue de Sèvres, 75007 Paris, lebonmarche.com

This iconic department store embodies luxury and style. It's renowned for its elegant array of fashion, home decor, and gourmet food. The historic Le Bon Marché Rive Gauche is mostly frequented by Parisians, offering a distinct shopping experience.

Galeries Lafayette Champs-Elysées

60 Avenue des Champs-Élysées, 75008 Paris, galerieslafayette.com

Different from the 'classic' Galeries Lafayette, this building seamlessly blends modern and Art Deco elements. With four floors of shopping, featuring a fluid design, it effortlessly integrates a diverse range of items, from fashion and lifestyle to food.

Galeries Lafayette Haussmann

40 Boulevard Haussmann, 75009 Paris, haussmann.galerieslafayette.com

A Parisian shopping landmark: with its iconic stained-glass dome, Galeries Lafayette Haussmann might be the most famous department store in Paris. Don't miss the opportunity to visit the top floor for stunning views from the roof terrace.

Printemps

64 Boulevard Haussman, 75009 Paris, printemps.com

Next to Lafayette, you'll discover another luxury shopping paradise named Printemps. Go upstairs for a bite with a view over the city. This department store boasts an equally beautiful but just lesser-known stained-glass dome known as La Coupole Neige (the Snow Dome).

↓ LE BON MARCHÉ

BOOKSHOPS

Librairie Galignani

224 Rue de Rivoli, 75001 Paris, galignani.fr

Step into the refined world of literature at Librairie Galignani, Paris' oldest English bookshop. Established in 1801, this bookshop offers an elegant escape for book lovers, with a collection ranging from literature to art and fashion.

Smith & Son

248 Rue de Rivoli, 75001, smithandson.com

An independent English bookshop that was opened in 1870, Smith & Son caters to readers of all ages and offers a range of books and magazines across genres.

Librairie Gourmande

92-96 Rue Montmartre, 75002 Paris, librairiegourmande.fr

Satisfy your literary and culinary cravings at Librairie Gourmande on Rue Montmartre. This specialised bookshop caters to food lovers, providing an extensive selection of books on gastronomy, cooking, and the art of food.

Ofr.

20 Rue Dupetit-Thouars, 75003 Paris, insta @ ofrparis

Near Place de la République, Ofr. stands out as Paris' most avant-garde bookshop. In addition to being a bookshop, it is an independent publisher and art gallery, hosting monthly exhibitions. With varied collections of art, fashion magazines, and photography books, OFR. is a lively cultural hub.

Les bouquinistes de la Seine

Les quais de la Seine, 75004 Paris

Along the Seine, the *bouquinistes* (old green bookstalls) line the quays, offering vintage books, posters, and prints. It's a picturesque and literary experience while strolling along the riverbanks.

The Abbey Bookshop

29 Rue de la Parcheminerie, 75005, abbeybookshop.org

A Canadian gem in Quartier Latin. The Abbey Bookshop presents a vast collection that includes both new and used books, featuring around 40,000 English titles. It's housed in the historic Hôtel Dubuisson.

Librarie Majo

27 Rue des Boulangers, 75005 Paris, librairiemajo.com

Librairie Majo, a feminist bookshop in Paris, welcomes book lovers with its broad collection. Beyond books, this bookshop serves as a hub for discussions, celebrating feminist literature and ideas.

Shakespeare and Company

37 Rue de la Bûcherie, 75005 Paris, shakespeareand-company.com

Dive into the rich literary history of Paris at Shakespeare and Company, an iconic bookshop in the heart of the city. With a history dating back decades, this charming shop welcomes book enthusiasts to explore its cosy space, filled with a large range of books. It is a very popular destination, especially in summer there might be queue to enter.

Tram café-restaurant

47 Rue de la Montagne Sainte Geneviève, 75005 Paris

Tram café-restaurant offers a fusion of books and food. The cosy retreat invites you to enjoy both the written word and the flavours that Tram has to offer.

The Red Wheelbarrow Bookstore

11 Rue de Médicis No. 9, 75006 Paris, theredwheelbarrow-bookstore.com

Immerse yourself in the world of English literature at The Red Wheelbarrow, a charming shop catering to the English-speaking community. They offer carefully curated selections of novels, poetry, and non-fiction books.

San Francisco Books Co.

17 Rue Monsieur le Prince, 75006 Paris, sfparis.com

The San Francisco Book Co. is a literary oasis in Paris. The quaint bookshop specialises in rare and vintage editions, creating a nostalgic atmosphere to explore. The smell of aged paper and the charm of vintage covers make it a sanctuary for those who appreciate the tactile beauty of classic literature.

Assouline

35 Rue Bonaparte, 75006 Paris, assouline.com

A luxury bookshop with sophisticated design. Assouline specialises in coffee table books on fashion, art, travel, and more, creating an art gallery-like ambiance.

Artazart

83 Quai de Valmy, 75010 Paris, artazart.com

You can't miss the vibrant red façade of Artazart, a design bookshop known for its selection of design, fashion, art, and photography books. The occasional exhibitions add a dynamic touch, making it an artsy destination for book lovers.

Violette and Co

52 Rue Jean-Pierre Timbaud, 75011 Paris, violetteandco.com

Violette and Co is a one of a kind destination, offering a large collection of books ranging from cookbooks to themed travel guides about Paris. They also offer souvenirs such as posters, photo prints, and notebooks. Stop by at the coffee bar on the top floor for a drink.

La Régulière

43 Rue Myrha, 75018 Paris, lareguliere.fr

La Régulière is more than just a bookshop, creating a vibrant community hub where literature and social engagement meet. They organise exhibitions and art workshops, and set up encounters with authors and other speakers.

Librairie l'Arabesque

Centquatre-Paris, 5 Rue Curial, 75019 Paris

Librairie l'Arabesque adds a cultural touch to the Parisian literary scene by specialising in Arabic literature, providing a unique space for diverse literary traditions. It serves as a cultural bridge, promoting appreciation for Arabic storytelling.

Librairie Le Monte en l'Air

2 Rue de la Mare, 75020 Paris

A beacon for alternative literature in Paris. The shop stands out for its unusual selection and commitment to diverse voices. Librairie Le Monte en l'Air is also a cultural hub, hosting events and discussions.

Bookshop Palais de Tokyo

13 Avenue du Président Wilson, 75116 Paris, palaisdetokyo.com-bookstore.com

Spanning 450m^2, the bookshop in Palais de Tokyo offers an international selection of books, magazines, and unique items tied to their exhibitions.

ART SUPPLIES

Lavrut

52 Passage Choiseul, 75002 Paris, lavrut.com

With a broad selection of quality art supplies, from paints to brushes, Lavrut provides both seasoned and budding artists with a wonderful shopping experience.

Rougier&Plé

15 Boulevard des Filles du Calvaire, 75003 Paris, rougier-ple-paris3.fr

Offering a wide array of supplies, Rougier&Plé caters to artists of all levels. From sketchbooks to specialised tools, this store delivers on all your creative needs.

Lez'arts

24 Rue du Regard, 75006 Paris, lez-arts.com

Lez'arts in Paris is a lively art supply shop known for its quality materials and welcoming ambiance, catering to artists in search of inspiration and top-notch tools.

Boesner

46 Rue du Chemin Vert, 75011 Paris, boesner.fr

Boesner provides a vast range of high-quality supplies for painting, drawing, and crafting. Their commitment to artistic excellence makes it a preferred destination for creatives.

Magasin Sennelier

3 Quai Voltaire, 75007 Paris, magasinsennelier.art

Renowned globally, Magasin Sennelier offers a selection of high-quality art supplies. Explore pigments, brushes, and canvases, and let the essence of Parisian artistry inspire your creativity.

Le Géant des Beaux-Arts

166 Rue de la Roquette, 75011 Paris, geant-beaux-arts.fr

A giant in the art supply world, Le Géant des Beaux-Arts caters to various artistic preferences, providing a multitude of materials for painting, drawing, and crafting.

Passage Clouté

7 Rue des Boulets, 75011 Paris, passagecloute.com

The charming art supply shop Passage Clouté offers a carefully curated selection of materials, creating a unique and welcoming atmosphere for artists of all kinds.

Adam Montparnasse

24 Rue du Regard, 75006 Paris, lez-arts.com

With decades of legacy, Adam Montparnasse provides a range of art materials, making it a haven for artists seeking both classic and contemporary supplies.

AFFORDABLE ART & HOME DECO

Maisons du Monde

maisonsdumonde.com

Maisons du Monde, with multiple locations, offers a wide range of home decor. From vases and serveware to all sorts of knick-knacks, you'll find an assortment of stylish products that often reflect popular trends.

Merci

111 Boulevard Beaumarchais, 75003 Paris, merci-merci.com

Parisian concept store Merci provides stylish items such as serveware and candles, donating part of the proceeds to charities. Other reasons to visit are La Cantine Merci in the basement, and Merci Cine Café. The associated pizzeria Grazie is located at number 91.

Fleux

39 Rue Sainte-Croix de la Bretonnerie, 75004 Paris, fleux.com

Fleux in the Marais district has four shops on one street, offering a mix of items from posters to home decor. It's the go-to spot for interesting and stylish gifts with designs from both French and international talents.

La Mouette Rieuse

17bis Rue Pavée, 75004 Paris, lamouetterieuseparis.com

La Mouette Rieuse is a cultural concept store, blending a charming array of Parisian-themed items and a large collection of books. Alongside quirky souvenirs, visitors can enjoy a coffee on the cosy terrace.

Smallable

81 Rue du Cherche-Midi, 75006 Paris, smallable.com

Family concept store Smallable stocks a range of products, from fashion items to home decor, including decorative pieces and furniture. Pricing varies widely, ensuring there's something for everyone.

Centquatre-Paris (104)

5 Rue Curial, 75019 Paris, 104.fr

Centquatre-Paris is a cultural hub uniting different artforms and offering artwork for sale. Atelier Kiblind showcases posters by various artists, while eco-friendly shop L'effet PAP features beautiful items from environmentally conscious French companies. Land, a florist, offers flowers along with a variety of pots and vases.

↓ MERCI

↓ FLEUX

↓ MERCI

RECORD SHOPS

Superfly Records

53 rue Notre Dame de Nazareth, 75003 Paris, superflyrecords.com

Looking for rare and vintage vinyl? Pay a visit to Superfly Records. Explore the shelves and let the soulful beats guide your journey through this musical destination.

La Dame Blanche Record Shop

47 Rue de la Montagne Sainte Geneviève, 75005 Paris

La Dame Blanche Record Shop offers a charming space for music aficionados. Flip through their collection – each record tells a story – and you might uncover a hidden gem.

Paris Jazz Corner

5 rue de Navarre, 75005 Paris, parisjazzcorner.com

Paris Jazz Corner is a dedicated space offering a rich collection of jazz records. Immerse yourself in the world of improvisation and timeless melodies.

Ground Zero

114 Rue du Faubourg Poissonnière, 75010 Paris, groundzero.fr

Experience music in-store at Ground Zero. Take a moment to appreciate the tunes before making your selection in this incomparable auditory space.

Babaluma

72 bis Rue Jean-Pierre Timbaud, 75011 Paris, discogs.com

With vinyl prices starting at €1, Babaluma presents both new and vintage records. This affordable option in Paris draws those seeking budget-friendly musical treasures.

Comets Café & Disques

38 Rue Léon Frot, 75011 Paris, cafecomets.fr

Not only a record shop but also a coffee and lunch spot, Comets Café & Disques invites you to savour the notes of vinyl and the flavours of wonderful meals. Check their website for gigs during your stay.

Techno Import

16 Rue des Taillandiers, 75011 Paris, techno-import.fr

Delve into the electronic realm at Techno Import. Explore the beats and rhythms that define the genre in a shop that caters to the electronic music scene.

Balades Sonores

8 Rue Pierre Picard, 75018 Paris, baladessonores.com

Balades Sonores is a record store and cultural space. Occasional live performances add a dynamic element. Keep an eye out for the shop cat as you browse through the varied selection.

Le Rideau de Fer

12 Rue André del Sarte, 75018 Paris, lerideaudefer.com

Musical sanctuary Le Rideau de Fer attracts vinyl enthusiasts with its eclectic collection. Explore the methodical selection of records spanning genres.

TIGER MATCH
THE BEE
LUXURY
SAFETY MATCHES
MATCHBOXES
TIGER MATCH
THE HIPPOPOTAMUS
THE BEE
LUXURY
SAFETY MATCHES
THE WAVE
LUXURY MATCHES
LUXURY MATCHES

DYADE
ASPHALTE
POILS ET PLUMES
OUVERTURES
VICTOIRE ORTH

SHOPS WE LOVE

Deyrolle

46 Rue du Bac, 75007 Paris, deyrolle.com

Explore the extraordinary at Deyrolle, a shop known for taxidermy wonders and an extensive collection of natural history artefacts. It offers a captivating journey into the wonders of the animal kingdom.

↓ DEYROLLE

↓ DEYROLLE

Le Tampographe Sardon

4 Rue du Repos, 75020 Paris, tampographe.com

Explore the whimsical world of rubber stamp printing at Le Tampographe Sardon, specialising in quirky and artistic designs. The shop is filled with playful paper goods, from personalised stationery to curious creations.

Japan Arcade

1 Rue du Four, 75006 Paris, japan-arcade.com

Explore Japan's vibrant pop culture at Paris' Japan Arcade, a small shop celebrating gaming and anime that sells collectibles and rare finds for devotees and curious visitors alike.

L'Objet qui Parle

86 Rue des Martyrs, 75018 Paris, lobjetquiparle.fr

Explore the eclectic charm of L'Objet qui Parle in Montmartre, a quaint antique shop with a mishmash of taxidermy, candleholders, tableware, and more. It captures the bohemian spirit, inviting visitors for leisurely browsing.

Farman Aviation Antiquités

122 Rue du Bac, 75007 Paris, pierre-farman.com

If you're drawn to the allure of aviation history, Farman Aviation Antiquités is a vintage shop unlike any other. Specialising in aviation memorabilia, from antique propellers to vintage pilot's gear, the shop offers a glimpse into the world of flight.

Tienda Esquipulas

20 Rue Houdon, 75018 Paris, esquipulas.fr

Tienda Esquipulas brings Latin American flair to Paris with an eclectic mix of folk art, religious artefacts, and unique handicrafts. Take a cultural journey through vibrant and distinctive treasures in this one-of-a-kind shop.

GREEN PARIS

PARKS & SWIMMING

Jardin des Tuileries

Jardin des Tuileries, 75001 Paris

Nestled between the Louvre Museum and Place de la Concorde, Jardin des Tuileries is a landscaped garden that provides a serene setting for strolls. Its symmetrical design, fountains, and sculptures make it a delightful retreat.

Square du Vert-Galant

15 Place du Pont Neuf, 75001 Paris

Located on the western tip of Île de la Cité, this square offers a peaceful retreat. Its location along the Seine makes it a popular spot for a relaxing picnic while enjoying the river views.

Place des Vosges

Place des Vosges, 75004 Paris

While technically a square, Place des Vosges is surrounded by elegant arcaded buildings as well as gardens. It's the oldest planned square in Paris and a peaceful place to unwind.

Jardin des Plantes

57 Rue Cuvier, 75005 Paris, jardindesplantesdeparis.fr

One of the main botanical gardens in Paris, Jardin des Plantes is not just a beautiful collection of gardens; it also houses the Natural History Museum. You'll find a diverse collection of flora, including tropical greenhouses and thematic gardens.

↓ PLACE DES VOSGES

↓ JARDIN DU LUXEMBOURG

↓ JARDIN DES PLANTES

↓ JARDIN DES PLANTES

Piscine Pontoise

19 Rue de Pontoise, 75005 Paris, espace-sportif-pontoise-paris.fr

Swim in style at Piscine Pontoise, where elegance and luxury converge in a refined setting. Enjoy a unique swimming experience amidst architectural beauty and a delightful atmosphere.

Jardin du Luxembourg

Jardin du Luxembourg, 75006 Paris, jardin.senat.fr

Jardin du Luxembourg is one of the most beautiful and popular public parks in Paris, located near Quartier Latin. In the park you'll find Palais du Luxembourg, Luxembourg Palace, which nowadays houses the French Senate.

Champs-de-Mars

Champs-de-Mars, 75007 Paris

Champs de Mars is the perfect spot for an evening picnic with a stunning view of the Eiffel Tower. Good to know: this park is always open while other parks in Paris close after sunset.

Parc Monceau

35 Boulevard de Courcelles, 75008 Paris

This English-style Parc Monceau features charming bridges, statues, and a collection of architectural elements and statues.

Canal Saint-Martin

Canal Saint-Martin, 75010 Paris

The banks of Canal Saint-Martin offer a popular spot for leisure activities and picnics. The tree-lined pathways and charming footbridges create a serene atmosphere. A bit further down the canal you'll find Bassin de la Villette, the largest artificial lake in the city, where locals and tourists enjoy various water activities, including kayaking, paddleboarding, and swimming during Paris Plages in summer.

Piscine Oberkampf

160 Rue Oberkampf, 75011 Paris, piscineoberkampf.com

Discover the enchanting Piscine Oberkampf, a breathtaking Art Deco pool that, despite initial plans for demolition, continues to shine as a historical gem and a tribute to timeless design.

Bois de Vincennes

Bois de Vincennes, 75012 Paris

On the eastern side of Paris, you can find the largest public park of the city. Lac Daumesnil is a popular spot for recreational activities. Visitors can explore the Château de Vincennes as well, the mediaeval fortress in the park.

Promenade Plantée

Coulée Verte René-Dumont, 75012 Paris

Situated in the 12th arrondissement, Promenade Plantée, an elevated park on the Viaduc des Arts, offers a quiet retreat with tree-lined paths and greenery. The Viaduc des Arts houses art galleries and artisan workshops, adding a dash of artistry and culture to this urban oasis.

Piscine Joséphine Baker

Quai François Mauriac, 75013 Paris, piscine-baker.fr

Piscine Joséphine Baker, a floating pool on the Seine, offers a unique swimming experience with stunning views of the city. Please be aware that at pools in France wearing a swimming cap is compulsory and swimming shorts are not allowed.

↓ PARC DES BUTTES-CHAUMONT

↓ CANAL SAINT-MARTIN

Île aux Cygnes

Île aux Cygnes, 75015 Paris

This small artificial island in the Seine is known for its long tree-lined promenade and a replica of the Statue of Liberty. It provides a peaceful escape with stunning views of the river and the Eiffel Tower.

Parc des Buttes-Chaumont

Parc des Buttes-Chaumont, 75019 Paris

Characterised by its hilly terrain and extraordinary landscapes, this park is a favourite among locals. Parc des Buttes-Chaumont has a lake and an island with Temple de la Sibylle on top of the cliff, which offers amazing views.

Parc de la Villette

211 Avenue Jean Jaurès, 75019 Paris, en.lavillette.com

Parc de la Villette is a popular urban park known for its modern design and cultural importance. With its contemporary buildings, spacious lawns, and cultural spaces, the park provides a mix of recreational activities, educational opportunities, and artistic experiences.

Bois de Boulogne

Bois de Boulogne, 75116 Paris

Bois de Boulogne, on the western edge of Paris, is a forest with lakes, gardens, and even a horse racing track. Lac Inférieur and Lac Supérieur offer picturesque settings. Visit Parc Bagatelle and Fondation Louis Vuitton for some culture.

VEGETARIAN & VEGAN PARIS

La Cantine de Sam

Don't just walk past the cheerful blue façade of La Cantine de Sam! It is a delightful spot with an affordable and varied menu featuring vegetarian and vegan dishes, including bowls, Greek, Middle Eastern, and burgers. You can find it on two locations.

insta @lacantinedesam

Cojean

With multiple locations across Paris, healthy fast-food chain Cojean is a godsend for vegans on the go, providing a varied menu that also provides gluten-free options. The restaurant upholds values such as sustainable fishing, seasonal ingredients, organic produce, and fair trade.

cojean.fr

Judy Market

Focused on healthy eating, Judy Paris is a gluten-free restaurant with a lot of vegan choices, including options like scrambled tofu. Visit their charming location at 37 Rue D'Assas for a delightful terrace experience. They have three restaurants in the city.

judy-paris.com

Land and Monkeys

Treat yourself to vegan French pastries at Land and Monkeys, a renowned vegan bakery with multiple locations. They offer a delightful range, from vegan *viennoiseries* to savoury specialties like quiche Lorraine.

land-and-monkeys.com

Mamé Kitchen

Mamé Kitchen has a flexitarian approach, offering a vegetarian and vegan menu that is also gluten-free. While the focus is on plant-based options, a thoughtful selection of chicken and beef dishes are offered for variety. Three restaurants in Paris.

mame-kitchen.com

Maisie Café

A Parisian coffee shop that is both vegan and gluten-free, Maisie Café invites you to savour delightful treats in a cosy and conscious setting.

32 Rue du Mont-Thabor, 75001 Paris, maisiecafe.com

Maslow

A low-impact vegetarian restaurant with a menu featuring Middle Eastern and French cuisines. Maslow encourages dish sharing and embraces a sustainable dining concept.

14 Quai de la Mégisserie, 75001 Paris, maslow-group.com

Mopa

Mopa's lunch deal, priced at €15 on weekdays, includes a sandwich, fries, and a homemade beverage. Known for its vegan kebabs and 'fish' & chips, it's a lunchtime delight.

17 Rue du Croissant, 75002 Paris, mopa-concept.fr

Guenmaï

A place for healthy and vegan eating, Guenmaï focuses on macrobiotic and detox cuisine, also functioning as a tea salon.

6 Rue Cardinale, 75006 Paris, Insta @guenmai

Havana
Club

Le Potager de Charlotte

Run by two brothers, Le Potager de Charlotte showcases sophisticated plant-based cuisine using local, seasonal, and organic produce. With a refined interior and an extensive wine list with primarily organic options, it stands out in the world of vegan dining. In both the 9th and the 17th arrondissement.

lepotagerdecharlotte.fr

B.Better

A vegan tapas spot in Le Marais with Mexican influences, B.Better offers a changing menu with seasonal variations.

26 Rue Beautreillis, 75004 Paris, bbetterparis.fr

Mesa de Hoy

Immerse yourself in plant-based South American-inspired cuisine at Mesa de Hoy. They pride themselves on fair and locally sourced ingredients, working with small independent producers as much as possible.

68 Rue des Martyrs, 75009 Paris, hoyparis.com/mesa-restaurant

Soya Comptoir Bio

At Soya Comptoir Bio, everything on the menu is plant-based, primarily crafted from tofu and soy. Despite being slightly more expensive, the continuous service makes it convenient for any meal.

106 Quai de Jemmapes, 75010 Paris, soya-cantine-bio.fr

Bodhi Vegan

This quaint Southeast Asian eatery, mostly Vietnamese, transforms traditional meat dishes into flavourful vegan delights based on soy. Located near Canal Saint-Martin, it's a hidden gem.

23 Avenue Claude Vellefaux, 75010 Paris, www.bodhivegan.fr

Plan D – Dwich & Glace

Satisfy your sweet cravings at Plan D, where you can enjoy 100% plant-based ice creams and sundaes made with an oat milk base.

22 Rue des Vinaigriers, 75010 Paris, daimant.co

Zoé Bouillon

Canteen-style eatery, Zoé Bouillon offers daily changing menus with vegetarian and often vegan options at reasonable prices.

29 Rue du Faubourg Saint-Martin, 75010 Paris, zoebouillon.fr

Aujourd'hui Demain

Have a culinary adventure at Aujourd'hui Demain, a vegan ethical concept store in Le Marais. Treat yourself to American or Mexican delights, including burgers and mac & cheese.

42 Rue du Chemin Vert, 75011 Paris, aujourdhui-demain.com

Mala Boom

Mala Boom, a Chinese restaurant, crafts a 'spicy love story' with its signature dish, *Le Málà Xiangguo*. This customizable dish allows you to create your own shared meal, with options for meat or vegan, on varying spice levels.

42 Rue Jean-Pierre Timbaud, 75011 Paris, malaboom.com

Martha Pizze Amore

Martha Pizze Amore boasts an impressive selection of seven vegan pizzas, four vegan pastas, and two vegan Italian desserts.

48 Rue Richard Lenoir, 75011 Paris, marthapizzeamore.com

Mori Café

Go on a delicious journey at Mori Café, a vegan Japanese restaurant. Owner Julia has transformed her Japanese mother's recipes into a vegan feast. With a menu featuring five main courses and five desserts, each dish is thoughtfully crafted.

2 Rue des Taillandiers, 75011 Paris, moricafeparis.com

Restaurant Têt

Experience a taste of Vietnamese cuisine with a plant-based twist at Restaurant Têt in Le Marais: they provide vegan alternatives for every meat option on the menu.

10 Boulevard du Temple, 75011 Paris, restaurant-tet.com

VG Pâtisserie

VG Pâtisserie is a charming French bakery with a twist: everything on the menu – from croissants to *viennoiseries*, and pastries – is fully vegan. In addition, they offer a generous selection of gluten-free pastries.

123 Boulevard Voltaire, 75011 Paris, vgpatisserie.fr

Comptoir Veggie

Dive into the goodness of Comptoir Veggie, a coffee shop and cafeteria offering a regular restaurant menu with a twist – it's all vegan! From soups and hotdogs to sandwiches and buddha bowls, they've got it all.

75 Avenue Ledru Rollin, 75012 Paris, comptoirveggie.com

La Bonne Heure

Embrace La Bonne Heure for a mix of vegan and vegetarian options. While slightly upscale, the menu promises a delightful culinary experience.

72 Rue du Moulin des Prés, 75013 Paris, labonneheure.org

Season Square

Vegan enthusiasts can indulge in a variety of options, including vegan burgers, at Season Square. The menu also features a selection of vegan desserts.

3 Rue Louise Weiss, 75013 Paris, season-square.com

Bloom

Indulge in vegan sushi at Bloom, where creativity knows no bounds. While slightly on the pricey side, the enticing combinations, house-made vegan salmon, and truffle cream make it a worthwhile experience. Two branches in the 17th arrondissement.

bloomsushi.fr

Combo Alguement Bon

Dive into the world of vegan Japanese cuisine at Combo, where seaweed sourced from Brittany adds an authentic touch. With starters around €5 and main courses around €10, it's a budget-friendly option.

80 Rue la Condamine, 75017 Paris, insta @combo_alguement_bon

Giardino

Giardino offers visually stunning vegan pastries, a variety of macarons, and classic French *viennoiserie* – all fully vegan. Gluten-free options are also available.

147 Rue Cardinet, 75017 Paris, giardinoparis.com

Sweet Rawmance

With an extensive menu featuring Italian, Middle Eastern, *crêpes*, and burgers, Sweet Rawmance offers beautifully presented and richly flavoured dishes. Although a bit pricier, it's a dream for those craving a vegan brunch.

17 Place Saint-Pierre, 75018 Paris, sweetrawmance.com

La Recyclerie

La Recyclerie is not just a restaurant; it's a sustainable eco-friendly space that promotes responsible consumption. Enjoy plant-based options in an environmentally conscious ambiance.

83 Boulevard Ornano, 75018 Paris, larecyclerie.com

OUTSIDE OF PARIS

Paris is a good starting point for trips further away. With the TGV you can be in the culinary capital Lyon within two hours. Or discover mediaeval treasures and Gothic wonders in Rouen. At the coast you'll find the breathtaking cliffs of Étretat and a little further south you can visit the iconic Mont Saint-Michel, an abbey and village on an island in the sea. We'll give you a few suggestions somewhat closer to Paris, all accessible by public transport.

Château de Versailles

Place d'Armes,
78000 Versailles,
chateauversailles.fr

The luxurious Château de Versailles stands as a testament to the grandeur of French royalty. Wander through its extravagant halls decorated with intriguing details and explore the expansive Gardens of Versailles with its beautiful fountains. Around 45 minutes by train. Free entry for under 26s.

Domaine de Trianon

Porte Saint-Antoine,
78000 Versailles,
chateauversailles.fr

Explore Domaine de Trianon, a peaceful retreat within the larger Versailles estate. Discover Le Grand Trianon, a pink marble palace, and Le Petit Trianon, a charming retreat built for Marie Antoinette. Stroll through the picturesque gardens surrounding these elegant buildings. 45 Minutes by train, free entry for under 26s.

Jardins de Monet

84 Rue Claude Monet, 27620 Giverny, fondation-monet.com

Transport yourself into the world that inspired Claude Monet's iconic masterpieces. The Jardins de Monet in Giverny burst with vibrant colours, featuring the famous water lilies, a Japanese bridge, and enchanting flower-lined pathways. You can also visit Monet's house and atelier. Around 75 minutes by train and bus. Reduced fee for students.

Musée départemental Albert-Kahn

2 Rue du Port, 92100 Boulogne-Billancourt, albert-kahn.hauts-de-seine.fr

Visit the Musée Albert-Kahn in Boulogne-Billancourt for a fascinating journey through early 20th-century cultures, captured in photos and films. Take a serene break in the Albert Kahn Japanese Garden, providing a peaceful escape just outside the city. This hidden gem reflects Japanese aesthetics, offering tranquil landscapes, wooden bridges, and peaceful ponds. Around twenty minutes by train and bus. Free entry for under 26s.

Château de Fontainebleau

Château de Fontainebleau, 77300 Fontainebleau, chateaudefontainebleau.fr

Immerse yourself in history at Château de Fontainebleau, a former royal residence showcasing rich architectural heritage. Explore the big Fontainebleau Forest, offering a delightful blend of historical charm and natural beauty. Around forty minutes by train. Free entry for under 26s.

Basilique de Saint-Denis

1 Rue de la Légion d'Honneur, 93200 Saint-Denis, saint-denis.monuments-nationaux.fr

Uncover the mediaeval history of France at the Basilique de Saint-Denis. Enjoy its impressive Gothic architecture and explore the final resting place of numerous French monarchs, making it a site of cultural and historical significance. Around twenty minutes by metro. Free entry for under 26s.

Château de Sceaux

Allée d'Honneur, 92330 Sceaux, domaine-de-sceaux.hauts-de-seine.fr

Find tranquillity at Château de Sceaux and its vast park. Admire the classical French gardens, characterised by their elegance and symmetry, providing a serene escape from the bustling city. Around thirty minutes by train. Free entry for under 26s.

Château de Rambouillet

Château de Rambouillet, 78120 Rambouillet, chateau-rambouillet.fr

Visit Château de Rambouillet, a former hunting lodge turned presidential residence. Explore its beautiful gardens and the scenic Rambouillet Forest. La Laiterie de la Reine and La Chaumière aux Coquillages in the English gardens are absolute must-visits. Around thirty minutes by train. Free entry for under 26s.

Musée Rodin de Meudon

19 Avenue Auguste Rodin, 92190 Meudon, meudon.musee-rodin.fr

Located in the quiet suburb of Meudon, Musée Rodin is a nice getaway dedicated to the works of the famous sculptor Auguste Rodin. You can explore his house, atelier, and garden filled with his masterpieces. Around thirty minutes by train. Free entry.

Arboretum de la Vallée aux Loups

102 Rue de Chateaubriand, 92290 Châtenay-Malabry, vallee-aux-loups.hauts-de-seine.fr

The Arboretum de la Vallée aux Loups, located in Chatenay-Malabry, is a peaceful botanical garden famous for its extensive collection of plants and trees. Walk around the peaceful pathways and themed gardens. Around 45 minutes by train and bus. Free entry.

Château de Monte-Cristo

Chemin du Haut des Ormes, 78560 Le Port-Marly, chateau-monte-cristo.com

Step into the world of Alexandre Dumas at Château de Monte-Cristo in Port-Marly. This small, but elegant, *château*, once Dumas' retreat, offers a glimpse into the life of the famous author of *The Three Musketeers*. Around 45 minutes by train and bus.

INDEX

ABOUT THE AUTHORS

Floren Bout

Floren considers herself a Paris expert. After several city trips and six months of studying in this beautiful city, she has seen almost every corner. From wandering around museums to strolling through parks and from having drinks in cafes to browsing shops, the streets of Paris are where she feels most at home. Where she can leave the city herself, Paris never leaves her.

Gaby Dingena

Gaby, a passionate Paris enthusiast, came to the city for an exchange programme. After falling head over heels for a Parisian, she made the bold decision to stay in Paris. Exploring the city by bike is her favorite hobby, capturing its architecture, street art, museums, and vibes of different neighborhoods with her camera. Gaby embraces the French *joie de vivre*, especially through the *apéro* – the quintessential French tradition of enjoying pre-dinner drinks with loved ones.

WHY SHOULD I GO TO PARIS
the city you definitely need to
visit before you turn 30 (or 130)

Published in 2024 by mo'media
P.O. Box 359, 3000 AJ Rotterdam,
The Netherlands, momedia.nl

Concept
mo'media

Text and address selection
Floren Bout & Gaby Dingena

Art direction and illustration design
Jelle F. Post

Editing
Ezra van Wilgenburg

Photography
Dani van Oeffelen, Vincent van den Hoogen, Petra de Hamer, mo'media BV, and others

Special thanks to
Maaike van Steekelenburg, Lotte Leeuwis, and Eva van den Berg

MIX
Paper from responsible sources
FSC® C014138
www.fsc.org

WHY SHOULD I GO TO?
Information on all our travel guides on **WHYSHOULDIGOTO.COM**

First reprint, 2025

Why Should I Go To Paris
ISBN 978 94 93 338 081
NUR 510

Disclaimer
The points of interested mentioned in this travel guide have been selected by the authors. None of them have been paid for inclusion in this book: the *Why Should I Go To* book series is entirely ad-free.

Publisher's Note
Every effort has been made to ensure that the information in this book is accurate at the time of going to press. The publisher welcomes any information or suggestions for correction or improvement. Please send us an e-mail at info@momedia.nl or a DM on Instagram.

whyshouldigoto

Why Should I Go To travel guides are available for the following cities: Amsterdam, Antwerp, Barcelona, Berlin, Budapest, Copenhagen, Dublin, Lisbon, London, Paris, Prague, Rome, Rotterdam a Valencia. More cities will be added soon.